WHO STANDS FAST?
DISCIPLESHIP IN DIFFICULT PLACES

Also by Michael Duncan:
Move Out (1984)
A Journey in Development (1987)
Costly Mission (1996)

WHO STANDS FAST?
DISCIPLESHIP IN DIFFICULT PLACES

MICHAEL DUNCAN

First published 2005
by Urban Neighbours Of Hope
PO Box 89
Springvale Vic 3171
Australia

© Michael Duncan 2005

Design: Brett Gosbell & Nick Wight

Unless stated otherwise, the scripture quotations in this book are from the New Revised Standard Version Bible, copyright 1989 by the Division of Christian Education of the National Council of Churches of Christ in the USA. Used by permission. All rights reserved.

National Library of Australia Cataloguing-in-Publication

Duncan, Michael Ian.
Who stands fast? : discipleship in difficult places.

Includes index.
ISBN 9780958060233

1. Christian life. I. Title.

248.4

ABOUT THE AUTHOR

Michael Duncan as a young New Zealander caught a vision for the needs of the world. In his early twenties he was converted out of the drug culture and eastern mysticism. After two years of Bible College training in Australia he pastored a growing church in Dunedin before responding to the needs of the third world himself.

In 1985 he and his wife, Ruby, with their two children relocated to the Philippines and moved into the very heart of a third world squatter community. For many years they lived and worked among the poor. Michael soon became the Team Leader of the work in Manila. Their concern was to bring about holistic transformational development and this necessitated being fully engaged in relief work, community development, social justice, evangelism and church planting.

In 1994 the Duncans returned to New Zealand and since then Michael has continued to be involved in urban work both in Australia (Melbourne) and New Zealand (Auckland). He has been a Senior Pastor of churches in both of those cities.

Since 1976 Michael has also been a speaker in many countries of the world. His own personal testimony, his involvement amongst the very poor of the world and his gifts in communication have taken him to many different groups and places as a communicator. By way of example, last year whilst in Fiji he was invited to speak to the elite group of soldiers imprisoned in Suva who were caught up in the recent coup in that country. And then just recently he had the privilege of speaking to over 100 Hindu students, many of them lepers, whilst in India. And then, very recently, he had the opportunity to speak at a special memorial service in Australia for some of the victims of the Bali tragedy in Indonesia. Michael is often asked to speak at youth conferences, churches and mission gatherings.

Michael has written three books. *Move Out* (1984) published in the United Kingdom was a call for churches to be involved in the wider world. A Journey in Development (1987) was a reflection on how followers of Jesus could best work amongst the poor. And *Costly Mission*, published by MARC in the United States was voted one of the ten most outstanding books in Mission in 1996. Michael has studied theology and sociology, and has also done work in Ethics and Development Studies at Oxford University. He has recently completed post-graduate research into the life of the German activist, Dietrich Bonhoeffer with the Tyndale Graduate School of Theology.

Currently Michael is a 'Portfolio Worker' where he is on contract with a number of organizations assisting them in their strategic direction, leadership and communication. Michael also runs a gap year called 'interMission' for those wanting to prepare for work, mission or further study at Carey Baptist College in Auckland, New Zealand. He is also a visiting lecturer at a number of colleges in NZ, Australia and elsewhere. His particular passion continues to be as a speaker, calling people and groups to be all that they were created to be and do.

ACKNOWLEDGEMENTS

In many respects the genesis of this little booklet was I like to think, a 'God thing.' I last wrote a book in the mid-nineties and have thus waited ten years before doing it again. This is how it came about. One night I received a bizarre little dream. In the dream a pencil had got stuck in my throat and I was desperately trying to choke it out. And then I awoke. I turned to Ruby my partner in marriage, shook her so that she was fully present to the moment and then told her of my little dream. "How strange," she muttered and then drifted back to sleep.

A few weeks later a possible interpretation of the dream dawned on me. Maybe, it was time to begin to write the things that over the past ten years I had been speaking about. Thus the pencil (writing) in the throat (speaking). But of course, in small New Zealand at the bottom of the world there is a problem with finding a publisher. I made this a matter of prayer and two hours later I received an email from Ash Barker. In it he asked if I could write up into a book some talks I had given at UNOH's 2004 Surrender Conference. Ash is the founder of UNOH (Urban Neighbours of Hope) and he also spoke at the conference, along with Tony Campolo. Not only that, but in the email he also said that he would like to help get it published in Australia. I took the coincidence of my prayer and his email as a sign to begin writing.

And so, I am indebted to Ash and UNOH for this venture. I have traveled with UNOH since its beginning and have been overwhelmingly challenged and moved by their commitment to both Jesus of Nazareth and to the poor of Australia and Asia. This little booklet is but just a small step in our common journey together.

I am also supremely indebted to the scholar/pastor Gregory Boyd. More than any other writer it was his books that steered me in the direction of this book. I was so impressed by his work that I have taken it much to heart. In this book I have sought to give credit where credit is due and have thus appropriately referenced his input. But more than likely I have failed to do this enough and there may appear sentences of mine that come too close to what he wrote. I can only explain this as someone who took his material to heart but I do ask for forgiveness if I have committed this error.

Another miracle along the way was a chance encounter with an editor here in Auckland, New Zealand. As a result we commissioned Keith Newman to tidy up my awkward way of putting things.

As to the title of this book, I am indebted yet again to Dietrich Bonhoeffer. On the very last day of having to come up with a title I happened to read his phrase 'Who Stands Fast?' in two separate books. Admittedly it is old English, but I think it captures the heartbeat of the book. And as for the cover, I am indebted to my sister-in-law Rachel Campbell. She is a professional artist who has sold work in New Zealand, Australia, Europe and elsewhere. We loved her cover the moment we saw it. And a final thanks to Brett, Nick and the UNOH Publishing team who made the production happen.

Please feel free to contact me through the following addresses:

micduncan@woosh.co.nz
www.michaelduncan.org

Mick

CONTENTS

CHAPTER ONE	DARK FOREST MOMENTS
CHAPTER TWO	IN THE WAR ZONE
CHAPTER THREE	BATTLEFIELD NIGHTMARES
CHAPTER FOUR	PRAYER AS A WEAPON
CHAPTER FIVE	ORDER OUT OF CHAOS
CHAPTER SIX	DEALING TO DUALISM
CHAPTER SEVEN	THE COURAGE TO STAND
CHAPTER EIGHT	REDISCOVERING OUTRAGE

CHAPTER ONE

DARK FOREST MOMENTS

My parents had just separated. That left us three kids at home with our mother and a journey ahead to move from Invercargill in the deep South Island to Wanganui in the North Island of New Zealand. We moved into a big two-story house overlooking a deep lake. Just down the road there was a cluster of about fifty pine trees but for a small seven-year-old, it was one of those forever forests, seemingly stretching for miles. One day I got utterly lost in the tall timber. Reduced to tears I screamed for help and to my boyish embarrassment it was a 10-year-old girl that came to my rescue. She took me by the hand and led me out of my dark forest.

I still have a hopeless sense of direction forty plus years on. Worse than that, my life has continued to be filled with dark forest moments. As the years have rolled by so have the disappointments piled up in my life. Time and time again, I found myself stapled to a spot screaming for help.

British essayist Frank W. Boreham tells of Hamilton Hume who led a band of explorers who trekked across Australia looking to find a route from Sydney to Melbourne. On the verge of exhaustion they pleaded to turn back but Hume, pointed to a mountain, confidently declaring that beyond that point was their hoped for destination. They marched on, eventually clawing their way to the top of the range. What they saw was devastating. There was no ocean in sight, only more cruel mountainous country to cross. They named the mountain on which they sat Mount Disappointment.[1]

Writer Gordon McDonald relays an encounter with an employee who came to see him. When he arrived, it was evident that he was highly agitated because a job he sought had been given to another. He recounted how he got the news, and as he did, it became increasingly clear that larger, longer-term issues about his whole life, not just this job, were surfacing. This event was the proverbial straw that broke the camel's back. There wasn't an ounce of vital optimism evident in his life. Soon he was weeping, strong wrenching sobs, and a great, great inner sorrow began to disclose itself.

After sitting quietly for a while, I said, 'Tell me where these tears are coming from.'

When he could gain enough control, he responded, 'I'm just so disappointed. So disappointed.'

'Disappointed in what?' I whispered. But deep in my intuitive self, I already knew the answer.

'In everything. I've had dreams and high hopes all my life. And nothing...nothing has ever turned out the way I expected. Jobs fall through; friendships don't make it; I feel as if I've flunked as a husband and father. My Christian life stinks. Nothing...nothing works'.[2]

These days, it's not hard for me to bring a tear to the surface. All I have to do is turn the pages of my memory. To begin with there was the awful silence between my parents that was eventually broken in divorce. A failed attempt at university followed, more specifically I was expelled and told never to return to any university in New Zealand until I was 25. Drug induced states during exam times didn't help but the deserved expulsion was a major setback. Becoming a follower of Jesus didn't exactly stem the flow of disappointments. In fact, it feels like I have had more hurt and pain since I met the Saviour than I ever did previously. The only job I could score after salvation was making glue in a paper bag factory. My prospects picked up and I found myself at a Bible College in Australia but then I got the terrible news that my 15-year-old brother had died in a motorbike accident. I refused to believe what my father had just told me over the phone. Just like in the movies, I dropped the phone, stormed out of the building and ran for miles.

Turning the pages, we come to the first church where I was appointed assistant pastor. Only nine months into the ministry, my wife and I were summoned to the home of the senior pastor who along with his wife proceeded to scream and swear at us. We resigned immediately. Within three years we had flown to the Philippines to a very different life in the heart of a squatter slum in Manila. We were there to serve the poor and follow the example Jesus had modelled. It was hellish. No one should ever have to live in an environment like this, not the poor or missionaries. In my first few years I got dengue fever three times and amoebic dysentery, as well as all the other relatively minor things like diarrhoea and worms. Then two years into our radical mission our third born, Joseph, died. A further two years in we had to close down much of our ministry due to mistakes we had made.

After all this mission madness we decided to take time out to study in Oxford, England. I studied theology and ethics at the university and also did a course in development studies at an institute. It was an enriching time. Oxford was like heaven. I dressed up like a penguin (long dark suit and white bow tie), sat their exams and even managed to pass with merit. However, after two years of costly effort, both in time and money, I was advised the qualification could not be conferred because of some administrative procedural requirements at Oxford. This was another huge and bitter disappointment to add to my list.

We returned to Manila and for the next five years enjoyed a successful time of community development only to watch all our efforts literally go up in flames. A rich Chinese man wanted the squatters off his land and torched the place. Like a match in a matchbox the fire raced through the entire slum licking up everything in its path. Years of literal blood, sweat and tears were reduced to ashes and rubble.

In 1994, we returned to New Zealand, to live in Taita, a lower class area just outside of Wellington. We went there intentionally to see if we could cut it in a relatively poor community in New Zealand. This period however was to be another episode in the 'long dark night of the soul'. It was a time of angrily walking in the park, coming home late in the afternoon, sitting quietly at the dinner table, going to my bedroom, pulling the curtains, sitting quietly in a corner or lying in a foetal position on the bed weeping. Looking back now, I was burnt to a cinder. For nigh on 10-years I had given my all and had returned to New Zealand with nothing left in the tank. I was full of pain, still struggling to move on from Manila. Deep down I also suspected that we had left Manila prematurely. An awful disempowering doubt was festering away inside of me. Had we made a terrible mistake in leaving the Philippines? The two years in Taita was a wilderness time. Even though I knew God did some of his best work in the wilderness, I found it extremely disorientating. It was a time of not knowing. Everything familiar seemed out of reach but I was determined to do my time so gave myself to it.[3]

Finally, two years later, a new chapter opened up for us and we moved again, this time to the inner city of Melbourne, Australia. We were under the impression we were being asked to pastor a church committed to Christ and the poor of that city. However, the familiar early warning bells of disappointment could be heard in the distance within two short months. One of the senior leaders in this church was a practising homosexual with a live-in partner. In a very veiled sort of way we had been told that there were some in the congregation who were gay. I did not mind that, what was unclear and unsaid was whether they were practicing or not. Once it became clear, I made homosexuality my hot topic of research for some months. This involved reflecting on what social sciences and scripture had to say, what other groups including the homosexual community were saying and finally what some of my advisors were saying.[4] I came to a position that was accepting of homosexuals but required me to argue that since the church was Christ's and not just ours, then it was up to Christ not culture to determine this. Put simply, it seemed to me that the scriptures prohibited practicing homosexuality in the same way that Jesus spoke against greed and materialism. I argued that a leader in Christ's Church could neither be a practicing liar, materialist or homosexual. I did not want to prioritise one habitual sinful practice over another.

The position I took came as a major disappointment to many of the good people in this church. They pressed us to accommodate the practice of the senior leader. Compassion pleaded that I stand alongside these people but faithfulness to truth, as I understood it, forced me to tender yet another reluctant resignation. My wife and I sat our three children down and informed them of this turn of events and that we would again be returning to New Zealand. They dissolved into tears at the thought of more disruptions in their lives. That night I got a letter from one of my children declaring hatred for me and God.

Arriving back in New Zealand I took up a role as the senior pastor of a middle sized church. There is no other way of describing it, but the next five years working in that church was like wading through cement. The place and the people reduced me to tears twice a week. Eventually I could see that it was killing me. Initially it was 'do-able but difficult' but within a few years it had become destructive. I was dying a thousand deaths daily and the lights were fast going out inside me. Yet again, there seemed little option but to resign.

Understandably, this final episode raised a few questions about me. Was I somehow fundamentally flawed? I sought out a counsellor and gave him permission to ask me whatever about whatever. Some months later he informed me his church was looking for a pastor and would I like to consider it? I wasn't up to doing another church but I did thank him for his vote of confidence. Extending this invitation was his way of saying, that what had happened to me in my life so far wasn't necessarily a commentary on me. Regardless, I was still left with the burning question: how do you explain the seemingly wasted years and the dark forest moments? This was my life and more to the point I had been trying to live it as a follower of Jesus. Why should I have faced more pain and suffering as a Christian than I ever did as an unbeliever? Is that the way it is meant to be? A friend of mine once said, "Michael, I have to admit it, we all do it hard but you've done it harder than most."

THE AGONY OF IT ALL

You don't have to look far to find stories that make mine pale. Walter Ciszek, was a young man with a big dream. He wanted to be a missionary priest to the Catholic communities of Russia. He did his training and upon graduation asked the Jesuit Order to send him to Russia. Instead his superior sent Walter to Poland. Philip Yancey picks up the story,

A few years later, war broke out and Hitler's army invaded Poland. In the horde of Polish refugees fleeing toward Russia, Ciszek saw a providential opportunity. Disguising himself as a worker, he joined the refugees and sneaked into Russia, where he had always wanted to serve. His prayers had been answered, he believed. Not long afterward, though, the Soviet secret police arrested Ciszek. The next five years, he was kept in Moscow's notorious Lubianka Prison, undergoing constant harassment and interrogation. In solitude throughout his time in Lubianka, Ciszek spent day and night questioning God. Where had he gone wrong? He had felt called as a priest, but how could he serve in solitary confinement? What use was all his training? Why was he being punished? Finally, he caved in to KGB demands and signed a written confession of spying activities. When he refused to cooperate further, he received a sentence of fifteen years hard labour in Siberia. In the Gulag's much harsher conditions of fierce cold and fourteen-hour working days, Ciszek got at last the chance to serve as a priest, after gradually winning the confidence of Ukrainian Catholics.[5]

We may celebrate the conclusion of the story but how do you explain the agonizing path to it? Take the story of a teenage boy who also had a dream that one day he would be a prominent leader. But everything it seemed went wrong. His own brothers turned against him and sold him into slavery. Eventually he was purchased by a prominent family in a foreign city but again there were obstacles. He was falsely accused of rape and thrown into prison. His suffering lasted thirteen long years. His dungeon became one of disappointment and endless delays. Finally he was released from prison and believe it or not, became a Prime Minister. His name was Joseph, the son of Jacob.[6] So what of the thirteen terrible and tragic years, filled largely with hate, suffering, darkness, injustice, human failures and a lot of pain?[7] Like Walter, we might celebrate the final outcome of Joseph's story but what of those seemingly lost years?

And what of my little story? I had come to a point where I just didn't know how to interpret the path any more. On a good day, I would see it in a certain way, but on a bad day, those old feelings of resentment and despair clawed at my soul. For months I was locked in the interpretation wars. Finally, during Christmas 2001, it all came to a head. As I walked along a beach I found myself involuntarily dissolving into tears. I knew I had to bring my past to closure but just didn't know how. On arriving home I went to my bedroom and got down on my knees to ask for guidance. Then, in the quiet, in one still moment, there was an answer, a voice: "Michael, just let it all go. Just let it go. Let the first half of your life go."

SETTLING IN SADNESS

Intuitively I knew to take this counsel seriously. I was reminded of Michal's story.[8] She was besotted with David. Who wouldn't be? According to one writer, he had "the fighting ability of a Navy Seal, the godly talent of M.W.Smith and the rugged good looks of a young Mel Gibson."[9] Now Saul, Michal's father, learned she had a thing for David and decided to use this for his own advantage. As a way of trying to control David he invited him to consider becoming Michal's husband. David was pleased to become the king's son-in-law. While we are told that Michal loved David we are never advised whether David loved Michal. They married but soon afterwards David fell out with his in-laws. His new father-in-law wanted him dead so Michal helped her man make his getaway.

Little did she know their separation would stretch to fourteen years and during that time relational hell broke loose. David, while hiding in the hills, scored a second wife (Abigail) and then a third (Ahinoam). So what was happening to poor Michal? Like a piece of furniture she was given to another man. In a sense Michal the princess becomes Michal the slave with no choice and no voice.

Many agonising years later, David finally wins the battle with Saul and returns home asking to see Michal. In response Michal is now taken away from the man she was forced to marry. Anyone would understand if she were angry, bitter, resentful and despondent. But it doesn't stop there. Despite being reunited with his first wife, David takes more concubines and wives – twenty in all! Now to celebrate his victory over Saul, he holds a party and in the middle of the street, almost qualifies as a streaker. He disrobes down to his boxer shorts. But before you get me wrong, this was all innocent. David, with an absolute sense of abandonment, was worshipping his God.

As David danced, Michal watched from her window[10] and a coldness crept into her heart, not due to the altitude but because of her attitude. Suffering can do that to people. She shut down, got stuck in her suffering and settled in her sadness. Let's add it up: she married a person who didn't really love her, she was abandoned practically at the altar, was forcibly given to another man, taken from him, and then forced to share her husband with other women. Michal had a right to feel hurt and abandoned, to resent how the men in her life – her father and her husbands – had passed her around. And yet other men and women in Scripture, who were similarly mistreated, still managed to transcend their circumstances (ie. Joseph, Job, Esther, Mary). They didn't settle in their sadness. They didn't go cold and shut down, they refused to get stuck in their suffering. We don't hear of Michal again.

Somehow I knew I was in danger of settling in my sadness and becoming stuck in my suffering. The only way out was to: *let it all go*. On an emotional level it took me about two years to do that. A fellow New Zealander, Mike Riddell, expands on Jesus' words, "unless a kernel of wheat falls to the ground and dies, it remains only a single seed. But if it dies, it produces many seeds" (John 12:24):

The secret of life is to learn how to die. Dying is an act of leaving behind that which has been known and loved. For some it is a gracious release, for others a terrifying threat. It is the simple act of opening our hands to release hold of people, places and things – and it is at times unbearably difficult…young people embrace letting go, the older you get the harder it is. You do it cautiously. Some things which are let go of might never come back.[11]

In other words, what we're talking about is the practice of relinquishment, the sacrament of letting go. If you are a *Star Wars* fan, a puzzling question may have been: How did the young Anakin become deadly Darth Vader? On a plane to Asia, I chanced upon a magazine interview with George Lucas, the producer of the *Star Wars* series. Lucas writes, "He turns into Darth Vader because he gets attached to things. He *can't let go* of his mother. He *can't let go* of his girlfriend. He *can't let go* of things. You are on the path to the dark side, because you fear you're going to lose things."[12]

Scripture abounds with examples of good people being invited to let something go. Take the story of Moses who by all accounts must have been quite a volcanic sort of guy. At one point he is so rattled by the incessant grumbling of the Israelites that he loses perspective. Instead of doing what God had carefully asked him to do to get water out of a rock, Moses, in his anger, blows his top, strikes out and basically dishonours God.[13] For this public display of disrespect, Moses is told that he will not be numbered with those who will get into the Promised Land. He had given his life, and much blood, sweat and tears to get into the Promised Land. To now be told that the door to his dream was closed must have been a huge disappointment. From experience however, Moses knew there was only one recourse open to him – to get God to change his mind. On other occasions he had managed to accomplish this through prayer.[14] He did receive an answer to his many petitions but not the one he wanted to hear. God told him to never raise the issue with him again![15] In other words, Moses was to let go of the shattered dream.

Literature abounds with the call to let things go. T.S. Elliot writes, "The new growth cannot take root on ground still covered with the old, and endings are the clearing process."[16] Further, in my readings I chanced upon this insight, "What we call the beginning is often the end. And to make an end is to make a beginning. The end is where we start from." The Poet, Macrina Wiederkehr, writes: "So often in Autumn I want to go lean my head against a tree and ask what it feels like to lose so much, to be so empty, so detached." She continues: "I think I've met one person in my lifetime who was truly empty. I didn't ask her what it felt like, but I remember a quiet joy that seemed to permeate her spirit, and she looked free."[17]

Most of us don't do endings that well and try to avoid them. We must however, face them and then turn away from them, let them go. Once there were two monks travelling through the countryside during the rainy season. Rounding a bend in the path, they found a muddy stream blocking their way. Beside it stood a lovely woman dressed in flowing robes. "Here," said one of the monks to the woman. "Let me carry you across the water". And he picked her up and carried her across. Setting her down on the further bank, he went along in silence with his fellow monk to the abbey on the hill. Later that evening the other monk said suddenly: "I think you made an error, picking up that woman back on our journey today. You know we are not supposed to have anything to do with women, and you held one close to you! You should not have done that". "How strange," remarked the other, "I carried her only across the water. You are carrying her still."

LOOSE LITTLE THOUGHTS

Are we still carrying things? Is it time to let them go? This is where I got to after the first twenty five years of doing life and ministry with Jesus. I still didn't understand it all, but knew I had to let it all go. This was no easy thing to do. There was no magic wand, no set formula, to suddenly transform me. It took nigh on two years before I felt I had unloaded most of the stuff. For each of us, the key will be different. For me, it had to do with my thought life. After leaving Manila I felt like I was now on God's B Team and that became the loose little thought that de-energized me and just about derailed my life. Let me explain.

Imitating Christ back in New Zealand became a matter of preparing meals for my family but no longer providing food for hundreds of malnourished Filipino babies. Imitating Christ became a matter of spending quality time with each of my children but no longer physically standing with the poor in their fight against unjust landowners. I was reduced to serving a few hundred people in a local church and missed walking through a densely populated Asian mega-city. I revelled in the drama and danger of living in the slums. It was like walking across a global stage of massive human need. Returning to New Zealand felt like slipping off the stage and tumbling into a world of lesser needs. To my shame I began to despise the small things that made up my world. I much preferred setting up preventative and curative medical centres for the sick and dying of the Third World to taking one of my own children to a local doctor in New Zealand for an infected scratch incurred during play. I preferred setting up banks and income generating projects for the unemployed and hungry in the Third World to cooking sausages and vegetables for my kids and wife in our suburban kitchen. I preferred marching with the poor as they protested over unjust evictions from their homes to faithfully mowing the lawns back home.

So despicable had these small things become in comparison to all that I had done in Manila that it wasn't long before I became quite depressed. I had experienced a severe bout of re-entry into New Zealand and grief over what I had left behind but there was also a slice of sin in this terrible time. My pride was hurt. I was no longer doing the things that were 'supposedly' important but had been reduced to peeling potatoes, cleaning dishes, and mowing lawns. I had gone from the places of destitution in the Third World to a pocket of suburban domestication in the so-called First World. From being an actor in the big world I had become a bit player and my pride felt this keenly. I felt like a has-been. Gone, it seemed were the days of being a history maker in the public eye. Back in New Zealand I had to grind through each day in a very private world on a very small local domestic platform. I felt I had been relegated to God's B Team and with this thought came the awful sense that I had somehow lost my way and missed the path to my destiny.

These thoughts tormented me and kept me bound. After reading a book by the Christian psychiatrist Archibald Hart,[18] I at last found some practical ways of controlling and directing my mental traffic. Further, I received a whisper of promise in my spirit one day that said: "Michael, out of your greatest mistake will come your greatest ministry and therein lies your destiny." That God could redeem me from this place of despair and put my back on the path to destiny seemed fantastic but it gave me hope. I began to hold the past more lightly but still often wondered why those twenty five years had been so hard? I still yearned for an interpretation.

1   From memory I think I noted this account from a book by James Emory White.
2   Gordon MacDonald, *Mid-Course Correction: Reordering Your private World for the Next Part of Your Journey* (Thomas Nelson Publishers 2000), p.10.
3   Early into this wilderness stretch, I joined all manner of groups and classes. I filled my week with so many activities. Eventually I came to see I was filling my life with 'replacement activity'. I was trying to replace Manila instead of facing up to the mistakes I had made there. So I thrashed about, swimming in all directions. I soon learned that it is during such dark times you have to learn how to be a floater. Thomas Green (*When the Well Runs Dry*, Ave Maria Press, 1979) writes, "The secret of floating is in learning how not to do all the things we instinctively want to do, to do the opposite of what our instincts tell us...to let go, hang loose, to float free...learning to float is counterintuitive." In other words, during this time, I had to learn how to be at home in the dark, sitting in silence or simply doing nothing; how to be at home in the sea trusting in God's current, Some worthwhile practices or habits to get into during these dark times are: (a) Find a regular time and place to be alone. (b) Begin a log of neutral zone experiences. (c) Write an autobiography – not to be published but to remind you of other chapters in your life. It is so easy to allow a wilderness time to sum up your life when in reality it is only one of

many chapters that will fill our lives. (d) Ask the question: what do you really want? (e) Think about what would be unlived in your life if it ended today? (f) Take a few days to go on your own version of a passage journey. This is where you go somewhere that helps you to own things, learn from them, and then relinquish them. Some people find a special trip to the sea or a mountain can help accomplish these things.

We must not treat ourselves like appliances that can be quickly unplugged from one situation and plugged in again. Rather, we must allow for the in-between time, the gap, the fallow time, the winter, the dark night of the soul, the time to drift.

4   I have found Richard Hay's (*The Moral Vision of the New Testament*, Edinburgh: T & T Clark, 1997) work on homosexuality very helpful. As a summary, he posits the following:
   (a) Can homosexual people be members of the Christian church? Well, can alcoholics be members of the church? We must learn to sit with those that we are in moral disagreement with. Having said that, the pastoral task of the church is still to call for the reshaping of a person in conformity to Christ.
   (b) Is it morally appropriate for Christians who find themselves having a homosexual orientation to then continue to participate in same-sex erotic activity? No! Jesus charged the woman to "go and sin no more." The sexual gratification of homosexuals or of anyone is not a sacred right.
   (c) Should the church sanction and bless homosexual unions? No!
   (d) Does this mean that persons of homosexual orientation are subject to a blanket imposition of celibacy in a way qualitatively different from persons of heterosexual orientation? Heterosexually orientated persons are also called to abstinence from sex unless they marry. Where does that leave the homosexual? Costly obedience, while "groaning" for the "redemption of our bodies" (Rom.8:23).
   (e) Should homosexual Christians expect to change their orientation? Without doubt there is a power that can transform the heart of a human person. That God can transform is not up for debate, but that God will in all people is less certain.
   (f) Should persons of homosexual orientation be ordained? If the person lived a life of disciplined abstinence and had the gifts and graces, I personally see no reason why not.
   (g) Should the church support civil rights for homosexuals? Yes! We must not single out homosexual persons for malicious discriminatory treatment. In the public arena we must do as Jesus did and protect the civil rights of people. In doing this we are not setting up homosexuality as a sacred human right.
5   Philip Yancey, *Reaching the Invisible God*, (Grand Rapids, Michigan: Zondervan Publishing House, 2000).
6   Genesis 37–50
7   David Seamands, *Living with Your Dreams* (Victor Books, 1990) p.164.
8   1 Samuel 16 – 2 Samuel 7
9   Liz Curtis Higgs, *Bad Girls of the Bible* (Colorado Springs: Waterbrook Press, 2001)
10 2 Samuel 6:16
11 Mike Riddell, Sacred Journey: *Spiritual Wisdom for Times of Transition* (Oxford: Lion Publishing, 2000).
12 'Dark Victory' by R. Carliss & Jess Cagle (*Time* magazine, April 27, 2002)
13 Numbers 20:1–12
14 Exodus 32:14.
15 Deuteronomy 3:23–26.
16 I gleaned this quote from William Bridge's book *Transitions: Making Sense of Life Changes* (Banner of Truth, 1979).

17 Macrina Wiederkehr, *Seasons of Your Heart: Prayers and Reflections* (HarperCollins 1991), p.7.
18 Archibald D. Hart, *Habits of the Mind: Ten Exercises to Renew Your Thinking* (Word Publishing, 1996). In this book Hart suggests a way to isolate, capture and replace loose thoughts that we might be having about ourselves, others, God or life. These loose little thoughts have the power to absolutely derail and de-energize us. To locate and liquidate them he commends the following practices or exercises:
  1. Thought Capturing:
     1.1 To discover the thought(s) that have precipitated a particular emotional reaction.
     1.2 To identify the thoughts preceding an obsessive ruminating thought.
  2. Thought Evaluating:
     2.1 To carefully analyse a thought and determine whether there is a reason for it and whether the emotion following it is justified.
  3. Thought Challenging:
     3.1 To remove the incapacitating consequences of a particular thought by challenging the underlying beliefs or assumptions of the thought.
  4. Thought Changing:
     – Repeat to yourself, as often as possible, a new thought to replace the old.
     – Decide what it is you want to believe and then believe it.
     – See a counsellor.
  5. Thought Preventing:
     5.1 To teach oneself to think more rationally during times of normal emotion and to practice healthy thinking.

CHAPTER TWO

IN THE WAR ZONE

Luke, the Gospel writer, tells of a horrific encounter between a boy and a demon.[1] The text actually infers that the boy has been ravaged by the demoniac since infancy. There are those who through dabbling in the occult open themselves to this realm and because of this are partly responsible for what has happened to them. This boy however, was innocent, unfairly targeted and cruelly taken advantage of. Further, he had been robbed of his speech and lost control over his body. An alien force had invaded his body. To put it crudely, the boy had been spiritually raped.

Here we see evil at its worst, when those already disadvantaged are further victimised. It is my belief that lurking behind Hitler and his Nazis were demonic forces. Dietrich Bonhoeffer, the German theologian who stood up to Hitler, wrote of his time, "How can one close one's eyes at the fact that the demons themselves have taken over the rule of the world, that it is the powers of darkness who have here made an awful conspiracy."[2] In the holocaust, innocent children were targeted, torn from their parents and tortured to death. Take, for example, the true account of what happened to a Jewish girl named Zosia:

> **Zosia** was a little girl….the daughter of a physician. During an "action" one of the Germans became aware of her beautiful diamond like dark eyes.
>
> "I could make two rings out of them," he said, "one for myself and one for my wife."
>
> His colleague is holding the girl.
>
> "Let's see whether they are really so beautiful. And better yet, let's examine them in our hands."
>
> Among the buddies exuberant gaiety breaks out. One of the wittiest proposes to take the eyes out. A shrill screaming and the noisy laughter of the soldier pack. The screaming penetrates our brains, pierces our heart, the laughter hurts like the edge of a knife plunged into our body. The screaming and the laughter are growing, mingling and soaring to heaven.
>
> O God, whom will you hear first?

What happens next is the fainting child is lying on the floor. Instead of eyes two bloody wounds are staring. The mother, driven mad, is held by the women.

This time they left Zosia to her mother...

At one of the next "actions", little Zosia was taken away. It was, of course, necessary to annihilate the blind child.[3]

I believe we saw this same demonic activity in the killing fields of Cambodia a few years back. I was taken to these fields, and more specifically to a huge tree in the centre of the field where I was shown five scarred shapes in the trunk. This was where five nails had been placed. In an horrific execution procedure the Khymer Rouge soldier would swing children around at such a height that their heads would smash into the nails. Cambodia taught me that even though humans can create much cruelty in this world, the sheer volume of evil demands further explanations. Like the child in Luke's account, the children in Cambodia, were not just the target of the Khmer Rouge but also satanic forces.

There is a spiritual rapist among us, roaming around forcing its menacing influence on people, especially the already disadvantaged and the young.

THE INFLUENCE OF AN ENEMY

My first real exposure to the things of the devil and demons came through a movie. In the opening scene there is an archaeological dig, interestingly in northern Iraq, near the ancient city of Nineveh. In the next scene a young Arab boy races through the market screaming, "They have found something". An old archaeologist has indeed found something. A small silver medallion with a picture of Mary and Jesus engraved on it. But as he searches through the rubble he also finds something else, an amulet – a small, greenish stone with a serpent carved into it. And thus we are given at the starting point of another tale of the battle between good and evil. As the archaeologist takes the two pieces through the marketplace all manner of weird events unfold, he stumbles and shakes, dogs fight and back in his office his previously reliable clock stops ticking.

The next scene takes us to a suburb in Washington, Georgetown. We are inside a typical house where a recently divorced mother is busy typing out a manuscript for her next book, but as she writes she hears strange noises upstairs. She walks the stairs where her 12 year old is asleep in her bedroom. The covers are pulled back and the window is open. The mother senses a coldness, a presence in the room.

These were the opening scenes of *The Exorcist*. At the time of my seeing the movie I was not a follower of Jesus and so understandably I came out of the picture theatre absolutely scared. There were Christians handing out leaflets and I grabbed as many as I could. Upon arriving home I began placing these pamphlets around my bed hoping that they would somehow protect me through the night. I then jumped under the blankets and sheets and lay still and sensitised to any creaking sound.

A few years later as part of the hippie drug counter culture I began to experiment with supernatural ways of seeking guidance. I tried Ouija and other types of boards, séances and other means of seeking otherworldly communications. I vividly remember one night when I heard a voice telling me to go to a particular city in New Zealand. The following day I packed my bags and there was first introduced to eastern meditation. Later at the time of my conversion to Christ I became even more convinced about the role of Satan. I found myself giving in and wanting to inwardly belong to this Jesus but I wrestled with that decision to let him take the lead and forgive me. Just as I made my commitment I suddenly found myself doubting all of it. What surprised and shocked me was the volume and intensity of those doubts. A whole truckload of them got dumped into my head. It was bizarre. Even though some of the doubts were rational, the sheer volume and timing of them was extraordinary. Something or someone did not want me to give myself over to this Jesus. To put it bluntly, I was battling an enemy. This episode reminds me of the parable of the Sower that warns of an enemy who will 'snatch away what has been sown in the heart' and stop at nothing to derail a potential disciple.[4]

It used to be that if you talked about devils and demons you had to lower your voice and whisper for fear of being seen as 'a crazy'. Today these topics are no longer spoken of in hushed tones. Hollywood is pumping out movie after movie on the demonic. The moguls behind these movies have discerned that a flood of so-called 'secular' people are turned on by tales of the dark side. Take for example, the movie about a naïve young man Kevin Lomax (Keanu Reeves), a lawyer, who gets whisked away to New York where he meets John Milton (Al Pacino). Milton takes the young lawyer to the top of a skyscraper building and says all of this can all be his. But the young lawyer's wife Mary Ann (Charlize Theron) gets spooked. Lomax eventually discovers that the smart, patient and cool Milton is in fact the Devil (*The Devil's Advocate*, 1997). Then there's the movie about priests who plan to kill a young woman Christine York (Robin Tunney) in the belief that Satan wants to get her pregnant so she can give birth to the anti-Christ. Jericho Cane, the hero of the movie steps into the madness and saves the woman and the world. Cane was played by none other than the current Governor of California, Arnold Schwarzenegger (*End of Days*, 1999).

In a recent poll in New Zealand, eight out of ten young people claimed to believe in the supernatural. Herein lies the irony, just when the so called 'secular' world is returning to the 'supernatural', the church is strangely quiet about Satan. And if some do talk about these evil forces of darkness, they frame it as structural evil rather than a personified devil. In other words, as their phraseology goes, what Paul had in mind when he was talking about principalities and powers[5] was not angelic beings but evil earthly structures. For sure, there is systemic and institutional evil. When we arrived in the Philippines, President Marcos was in power and if ever there was a case for structural evil it was during his rule. There is no denying institutional evil at the very highest levels of government and business. However, behind this evil, can lurk spiritual forces intent on wreaking havoc in people's lives and their communities. John Stott, tries to understand structural and supernatural evil in context:

> In reaffirming that the principalities and powers are personal supernatural agencies, I am not at all denying that they can use structures, traditions, institutions, etc for good or ill; I am only wishing to avoid the confusion which comes from identifying them. That social, political, judicial and economic structures can become demonic is evident to anybody who has considered that the state, which in Romans 13 is the minister of God, in Revelation 13 has become an ally of the devil....every good gift of God can be perverted to evil use. But if we identify 'the powers' with human structures of one kind and another, serious consequences follow. First, we lack an adequate explanation why structures so regularly, but not always, become tyrannical. Secondly, we unjustifiably restrict our understanding of the malevolent activity of the devil, whereas he is too versatile to be limited to the structural. Thirdly, we become too negative towards society and its structures....I want to warn against demonizing them [the structures].[6]

Ron Sider, Professor of Culture and History, echoes these thoughts of Stott's in writing:

> Both Jews and Greeks in Paul's day believed that both good and evil supernatural beings stand behind and powerfully influence social and political structures. Modern secular folk may find that hard to believe. But when I look at the demonic evil of social systems like Nazism, apartheid, and communism, or even the complex mixture of racism, lack of jobs, sexual promiscuity, drugs, and police brutality in American inner cities, I have no trouble at all believing that Satan and his gang are hard at work fostering oppressive structures and thus doing their best to destroy God's good creation. These fallen supernatural powers work to twist and distort the social systems that we as social beings need in order to be whole. By seducing us into many wrong choices that create evil systems, by

working against attempts to overcome oppressive structures and sometimes by enticing politicians and other powerful leaders to use the occult, these demonic powers shape our world. Evil is far more complex than the wrong choices of individuals. It also lies outside us both in powerfully oppressive social systems and in demonic powers that delight in defying God by corrupting the social systems that God's human image-bearers need.[7]

And finally, Heinrich Schlier warns us all when he writes:

> The enemies are not this or that person, nor one's own self – they are not 'blood and flesh'. Naturally, blood and flesh can be found on the front lines of this battle (cf. 2.3). But the conflict runs much deeper. The struggle is finally against a myriad of tirelessly attacking opponents, too slippery to grasp, with no specific names, only collective designations. They are superior to humans from the outset through their superior position 'in the heavenlies', superior through their invisibility and their unassailability. After all, their position is an all-pervasive 'atmosphere' of existence which they themselves generate. They are all, in the end, inherently full of deadly evil.[8]

NAMING THE POWERS

Whether we like it or not, there are forces that do not play by the rules, in fact they play dirty and are downright evil. Their one goal is to bring down the disadvantaged and the young. Of the 29 passages in the Gospels which speak of Satan, 25 of them are mentioned by Christ, the *One* Christians claim is the most in tune person that has ever lived on the planet. Not surprisingly, his followers also talked in terms of a personified devil. The apostle Peter described this Devil like a lion who roams around *looking for someone to devour.*[9] Just recently in New Zealand a mentally challenged person climbed over a zoo fence into a lion cage. Upon seeing the man screaming for help, the zoo wardens tried to lure the lion away but to no avail. Finally, they turned a powerful water hose on the lion which at least had the effect of keeping the beast away from the man and his rescuers. To say the least, the man was a 'bloody mess' after the ordeal. No one comes away unscathed from a lion attack. Besides being described as a lion, the Scriptures also define and name this evil entity in the following ways.[10]

1. Satan (Job 1:6–9; Matthew 4:10). This designation occurs 53 times in 47 verses in the Bible and it has the idea of 'adversary' or one who withstands. Satan is therefore a genuine opponent. James Packer, in his excellent reflections on the Book of Nehemiah, writes:

> The real theme of Nehemiah 4–6 is spiritual warfare, and Nehemiah's real opponent, lurking behind the human opponents, critics, and grumblers who occupied his attention directly, was Satan, whose name means "adversary" and who operates as the permanent enemy of God, God's people, God's work, and God's praise. Nehemiah does not mention him, but that does not mean that he was not there. Direct opposition on the human level to those who are obeying God, and the use of "flaming arrows" of discouragement (Eph. 6:16) to destroy hope, induce fear, and so paralyse their endeavours, are two of his regular tactics, and both are in evidence in these chapters. When you see Satan's fingerprints on events, it is a safe bet that Satan himself is actively present, even if he carefully keeps himself out of sight. We think of Satan as our spiritual enemy, and so he is, but we need to realize that the reason he hates humankind and seeks our ruin is because he hates God, his and our Creator.[11]

2. Lucifer (Isaiah 14:12). This name has the meaning 'to shine'. One way to entice someone to evil is to first make it attractive and appealing. This reminds me of a true but tragic story involving two unemployed men who, on September 13, 1987, in search of a fast buck, entered a partly demolished radiation clinic in Goianaia, Brazil. They removed a derelict cancer therapy machine containing a stainless steel cylinder, about the size of a gallon paint can, which they sold to a junk dealer for $25. Inside the cylinder was a cake of crumbly powder that emitted a mysterious blue light. The dealer took the seemingly magical material home and distributed it to his family and friends. His six-year-old niece rubbed the glowing dust on her body. And no doubt she danced in the dark allowing the glowdust to display her movements. The dust was caesium-137, a highly radioactive substance. The lovely light was the result of the decay of the caesium atoms. Another product of the decay was a flux of invisible particles with the power to damage living cells. The girl is dead. Others died or became grievously ill. More than 200 people were contaminated. Not all that glitters and glows is great! The things that shine may prove to be deadly.

3. Evil One (John 17:15; 1 John 5:9). The words that best define this designation are: vicious, degenerate, malignant, ugly, useless, injurious and destructive. Picking up on the last word, Packer again writes, "He (Satan) is not a creator himself, only a destroyer; he is a fallen angel, the archetypal instance of good gone wrong; and now he seeks only to thwart God's plans, wreck his work, rob him of glory, and in that sense triumph over him."[12]

4. Dragon (Revelation 12:7). To put it bluntly, the devil is hideous.

5. Tempter (Matthew 4:3; 1 Thessalonians 3:5). Bill Hybels suggests that this tempter comes to us wearing three hats. First as a tempter luring us to the forbidden. Then as a deceiver, whispering that we deserve the forbidden. And then finally as the accuser, in condemning us for taking the forbidden.

6. Belial (2 Corinthians 6:15). This strange name conjures up all that is worthless and brings about futility and eventual ruin.

7. Beelzebub (Matthew 12:24; Mark 3:22). To put it crudely, "the lord of the dung". This evil entity is intent on getting people, communities and nations into "the crap".

8. Abaddon, Apollyon (Revelation 9:11). Satan is the destroyer, intent on wreaking havoc in peoples' lives.

The Scriptures also use serpent, prince, god, spirit, rebel, liar, perverter and imitator and other designations to identify the fallen one and his attributes. How then does this section on devils and demons address the unanswered question: How do devils and demons help explain my past?

BRINGING THEOLOGY ALIVE

As mentioned previously, only nine months into our first church Ruby and I were called to the home of the senior pastor only to have him and his wife swear at us. Returning home, I quickly fell to my knees and asked for a heart that could forgive them. I also knew I had to resign. In 1985 we relocated to the slums of Manila, and set about trying to survive in a shack made out of loose plywood and corrugated iron sheets. The first four years I had dengue fever three times, amoebic dysentery and we lost our third born child. Ruby described those years as 'every day is a day in hell'. Half way through we took time out in Oxford, England, where I buried myself in two courses, one of which I passed with distinction but due to some sort of administrative misunderstanding the qualification could not be conferred. We returned to Manila and after another five years saw good work reduced to literal ashes and rubble. A rich Taiwanese man torched the place to get the squatters off his land. We returned to New Zealand where for two long years I grieved the losses in Manila. Then came what we thought was our next chapter, urban church work in Melbourne, but within several months we discovered the leading elder was a practising homosexual. Despite wanting to welcome and befriend the gay community I sensed certain lines had to be drawn. I was asked to resign which again plunged our family into crisis. For the next five years back in New Zealand I worked in a church that reduced me to tears at least twice a week. Those were years of wading through cement. In a nut shell, all of this bought an end to my first 25-years of ministry.

I believe God eventually showed me I had to *let go* of those years so as to not to be further embittered by them. It took a long time to do this and still I was left with the gnawing question of how to frame my understanding. These were years of tears, grief, death, losses, extreme hardship, bitter disappointments, betrayals, sickness, insomnia, and confusion. How do you make sense of them? What do you do with that? At last, I think I am beginning to see.

Early in 2004, I was fulfilling a speaking engagement in a New Zealand city and, true to form, visited a Christian book store. Once inside I am like a child in a toy store. My eyes morph into saucers; I salivate and relish each and every purchase. On this occasion, my eye caught the title: *God at War* by an author I had never heard of before, Gregory Boyd. As I was doing some post graduate research into the life of Dietrich Bonhoeffer, the German pastor who courageously stood up to Hitler even to the point of joining a conspiracy to assassinate Hitler, I was interested in issues of pacifism and violence. Without even scanning the sub-title, contents page or the price, I impulsively bought this book. Back home, settling into my bookish cave, I began to realise, to my absolute amazement that I had just bought a 413 page book on *spiritual warfare*.[14] I set about devouring this tome and so began a journey of discovery and the path to the profound explanation I had been seeking. This book began to theologically frame my story. I found it incredibly refreshing, insightful, liberating and theologically challenging. I have since bought just about everything Gregory Boyd[15] has written and sifted through it with a theological toothpick.[16]

Gregory Boyd served as a Professor of Theology at Bethel College in America for over 16 years. In 1992 he planted a church that now has over 5000 members. He is a pastor-scholar and theologian who sheds tears as he sits with ordinary folk whose lives have come unstuck in the maelstrom of life. There is a moral obligation amongst speakers and writers, to give credit where credit is due. You will soon discover how important his insights have been to me as you come across references and footnotes throughout the balance of this book. Boyd however doesn't come without some risks. In certain theological circles he is considered controversial. More will be said on this in chapter five, suffice to say that what I appreciated about him was his timely reminder about the warfare motif for present day discipleship.

GOD AND GODS AT WAR

At the centre of the universe there is an all powerful God who is without equal, without beginning and end. This God is absolutely good and powerful and deserving of our adoration and worship. However, this God is not the only power at work in our world. While not equal to him, there are other influences bent on using their power to cause mayhem and madness. God has chosen to create a world in which free will agents, both human and angelic, can and do run amuck. At times, these agents actually thwart the purposes of God. We read of the free will of 'experts' in Jewish law undermining God's purposes (Luke 7:30) and the apostle Paul being held back by rebellious angels (1 Thessalonians 2:18). In a daring act of self-limitation, not weakness, God chose to create a world in which even he would be limited at times by the free will of humans and angels. In his cosmos other entities have an influence and while God exercises control he has left us in many respects to the consequence of choices, be they from free will human agents or free will demonic angelic beings.[17]

In 1 John, for example, we read, that despite the triumphant resurrection of Christ, this present world remains under the control of the evil one.[18] Scripture refers to Satan as the 'god' of this world influencing all the kingdoms of this world[19] and boasting that he is ruler of this world. Again we see that 'fallen' free will agents can and do obstruct God's kingdom work. These forces of darkness are not just puppets on the end of God's divine string. At times they operate outside of and against his will.

Quite simply, for the past 30 years I have been in a war zone, caught in the crossfire of a cosmic war. As in any war zone there are causalities; bad things will happen to good people, and neat and tidy formulas do not always work. And in the war zone there is often friendly fire where you get shot by those on your own side. Boyd reminded me of all of this. Even though this deeper understanding will not bring back my son or take away 30 years of pain, the knowledge that I have been a Christ-soldier on active duty helps make sense of it all. Boyd's take on this warfare worldview inspires what he calls a sense of revolt. Like Jesus who opposed evil wherever he saw it, I too want to revolt against those forces that disadvantage the disadvantaged.

Despite the war wounds and the knowledge that new wounds will be added, I remain a Christ-soldier. For myself and Ruby, my partner in marriage, that means working in the trenches of the poorest part of our country with broken down, drug infested and domestic violent-filled families. For myself, I sense the Lord of Hosts would have me also be one of those sergeant-major types who travel around desperately trying to enlist others. As I have done so, my observation is that most Christians live as though we were in peace times with little of their lives reflecting the characteristics of Christ-soldiers in a war zone. Personal preferences rather than principles seem to dictate decisions. Discipline is a dirty word. Many a believer wastes many a night in watching stupid soapies on television. As for prayer, what is offered up is a rushed five minutes at the beginning of the day or a tired few minutes at the end of the day. Weekends are for leisure and pleasure pursuits. Houses are filled with the latest and the greatest. A lazy lifestyle marks the modern believer.

A Christ-soldier, on the other hand, will be marked by discipline. Personally I try not to watch any television Monday through Friday. This one act of self-control has freed up precious time for the war effort. A Christ-soldier will be a prayer warrior. Like Daniel, we are to be the kind of people who come into God's presence on a very regular basis (Daniel 6:10). A Christ-soldier will live simply so that others might simply live. A Christ-soldier will come to Christ with a "just say the word and I'll do it" mentality. A Christ-soldier will be passionate about evangelism, even on a holiday break. A Christ-soldier will be courageous about social action. Christ-soldiers are people of strong resolve who bite the bullet no matter what. They look out for their comrades-in-arms and ensure they care for and restore their own wounded.

As I have made the rounds, more often than not I have come under 'friendly fire' and 'theological flak' as I have described the war and made the call. Those on the 'Christian left' find it embarrassing to talk of devils and demons and much prefer notions of structural or systemic evil. They do not like talk of warfare or the use of military metaphor. My thoughts on the subject have at times got me into trouble with some Christians who believe my perspective is dated or too 'evangelical'. Those on the 'Christian right' are often troubled by the statement that even though God is without equal and in control, he is somehow at the same time not in total micro-control (see chapters five and six). Parents have been reluctant to let their children attend my lectures, conference attendees have prayed 'against me' while I have been speaking, and whole groups have stated they will boycott future conferences that have me on the agenda. While the number of opponents has been relatively small their opposition has been made all too clear.

1 Luke 9:37–43.
2 Quoted in Bob Bowen, "Driving Out the Demons," *Gospel Herald* 78, no. 20 (14 May 1985): 337.
3 P. Friedman, ed., *Martyrs and Fighters: The Epic of the Warsaw Ghetto* (New York: Praeger, 1954), pp. 166–67. Quoted in D. Rausch, *A Legacy of Hatred: Why Christians must not Forget the Holocaust* (Chicago: Moody Press, 1984), p.122.
4 Matthew 13.
5 Ephesians 6:12. At a scholarly level there is much debate and difference as to the nature of the principalities and powers. Some define the principalities and powers as structures in society like government, education, marriage and so on. All of these it is argued have been

created by God. However, when these structures gain independence from God and become autonomous and in a sense take on a life of their own, so they become destructive powers. The task of the church is to redeem these powers by challenging them and bringing them back under the Lordship of Christ. In other words, this view does not attach a separate heavenly entity to the principalities and powers. They do not have an existence independent of their material reality (Berkhof, Wink). This view has to all intents and purposes 'demythologized' the principalities and powers. A quite different view however, has continued to 'personalise' the powers. It is argued that the powers are demonic angelic free will agents. Such beings can exist even when not incarnated in matter (Boyd, Wagner, Kraft). For a very good treatment of these views and others see Thomas McAlpine's book *Facing the Powers: What are the options?* (Monrovia, California: MARC, 1991).

6 John Stott, *Ephesians* (Leicester, England: IVP, 1975), p.274.
7 Ronald J. Sider, *The Scandal of the Evangelical Conscience* (Grand Rapids, MI: Baker Books, 2005), pp.80–81.
8 Heinrich Schlier, *Der Brief an die Epheser: Elin Kommentar*, 7th. Ed. (Dusseldorf: Patmos, 1971), p.291.
9 1 Peter 5:8.
10 The following designations are gleaned from *Satanology: Our Invisible Adversary, the Devil* by J. Hampton Keathley III on the website – http://www.bible.org/docs/theology/stan/satano.htm
11 J. I. Packer, *A Passion for Faithfulness: Wisdom from the Book of Nehemiah* (Wheaton, ILL: Crossway Books, 1995), p. 93.
12 *A Passion for Faithfulness*, p.94.
13 Bill Hybels, *Faith in the Real World: Making Your Faith work in Everyday Life* (Hodder & Stoughton, 1982), pp. 190ff.
14 Gregory A. Boyd, *God At War: The Bible & Spiritual Conflict* (IVP, 1994).
15 See also, *Satan and the Problem of Evil, Is God to Blame, God of the Possible, Seeing is Believing*, and articles in *Divine Foreknowledge* (eds. Belly & Eddy), to name just a few.
16 Boyd has come in for some hefty criticism from some renowned evangelical heavyweights like William Lane Craig and Millard Erickson,. Their criticism is not polemic or reactionary but well thought out and comprehensive.
17 Some will take exception to this statement believing it compromises the character of God, and more specifically his omnipotence. That God is omnipotent is not being disputed, rather the nature and scope of his omnipotence. God can indeed do the miraculous but this is quite different from suggesting he can create circular squares or married bachelors. The Christian philosopher Alvin Plantinga writes, "most theologians and theistic philosophers who hold that God is omnipotent, do not hold that he can create round squares or bring it about that He both exists and does not exist…not even an omnipotent being can bring about logically impossible states of affairs or cause necessarily false propositions to be true" Alvin Plantinga, *God, Freedom and Evil* (Allen & Unwin, 1975), p.17. God having created freewill and given human and angelic agents the right to chose limits his willingness to interfere. This limitation is not a weakness but a self-limitation of God.
18 1 John 5:19.
19 2 Corinthians 4:4, Ephesians 2:2, John 12:31; 14:30; 16:11.

CHAPTER THREE

BATTLEFIELD NIGHTMARES

WAR IS HELL

Letting go of past disappointments and recommitting to the war zone is no walk in the park. It is always disheartening to see good people torn to shreds. In anyone's book, war is hell.

In 2002, I was speaking at a national denominational conference in Australia and in my first talk basically shared the personal disappointments outlined in this book. After my rather emotional message I sat down to gather my thoughts only to be gently interrupted by a kind looking man who asked if he could tell me his story. He had lost his wife to cancer a few years previously while she was still in mid-life. I thought that was the end of his story but with a deep breath he plunged into the rest. Only three months after losing his wife, his three teenage children were all murdered at a nearby park. I was absolutely stunned. This was a Christian family!

I gave my *Letting Go* talk at a church in Auckland and again it encouraged people to open up. A warm and loving couple told me about their family, and how they especially admired the one child of theirs that had become a follower of Jesus. She married a young Christian man and together they went on an overseas experience that included a walk in the wild side of the jungles of an African nation to see the gorillas in the forest. As they were guided into the forest a rebel army unit surrounded them and hacked their daughter to death with machetes.

I was told of Sally (not her real name), a Christian, in her teenage years who loved to attend church and hang out with the youth group. One night they decided to have a party at someone's place. As they danced about they were suddenly brought to a stand still by the sound of a screeching car outside. A few moments later leather clad gang members stormed the house and quickly isolated Sally and another girl. They then forced the both of them into the car and sped off. Sally knew she was about to be gang raped. As she had been raised in a Christian home, she prayed that somehow God would prevent what was possibly about to happen. The car did not miraculously stop. As they were dragged into a house, she prayed again for deliverance but no deliverer came. As she was being brutally raped she inwardly cried out to God to rescue her. He didn't.

Gregory Boyd, the theologian and pastor, tells two stories. The first concerns little Greta. She was an only child and so her Christian parents were quite understandably protective. Everyday they prayed for her protection. But then one day Greta was snatched from her neighborhood. Some months later her sexually assaulted, decapitated body was found in a plastic bag by a river bed. In one moment, life for this young girl and all who loved her, had became an unthinkable nightmare.

Boyd also relates the story of Laura:

> Several years ago a nineteen year old student I will call Laura confessed her feelings of guilt over the fact that she "just couldn't seem to truly trust God." In the course of our discussion I discovered that as a nine-year-old of an American missionary to Brazil, Laura had been raped by a missionary "friend of the family." She reported the man, and he was duly "punished" by being put on leave for several months and then relocated to another mission field! Young Laura was told that even "men of God" sometimes do bad things and need God's grace, just like everyone else. She was instructed immediately to love and forgive this man and not to talk about the incident to anyone. If God forgives and forgets, she was instructed, so must we.
>
> To make matters worse, as a typical (and unfortunate) means of comforting this victim, Laura's parents told her that God "always has his reasons" for allowing things like this to happen, though we of course may not understand these reasons until we get to heaven. Laura must simply believe that God was still "on his throne" and still "in control." She needed to trust God and believe that what the missionary intended for evil God intended for good. In time, she was told, she would actually be thankful for the experience.[1]

These are the sort of stories Christians want to keep to themselves and if possible hidden, for fear that if they got into the public domain they would be thrown back as proof that it is an absolute waste of time to believe and trust in God. These horror stories become the fodder of 'protest atheism'. They even have the awful potential to turn believers away from their faith. Sally for example, used drugs to dull the pain and eventually ended up as a prostitute to support her addiction.

A SOLDIER'S SCREAM

These are the nightmares of the war zone, horror stories we understandably do not want to hear, particularly when they happen to Christians who placed their trust in God to protect them. So what do you do with the frightening reality that God did not come through for these victims of the war zone when evil struck? What do you do when the casualties of war pile up and it is all too apparent that bad things continue to happen to good people?

Those who confess no faith in God use these stories to confirm their unbelief. It's ironic that when life is going well for atheists or agnostics they are so strident in their view that there is no God. When, however, suffering gatecrashes their lives, they are the first to rail against the very God they say does not exist. The movie of the life of Patch Adams (played by Robin Williams) is a case in point. The opening scene has Patch committing himself to a mental institution. He despairs over life and for his own protection puts himself away. While inside he gets a glimpse of another way of 'doing life'; being there for others, especially those whom no one else wants to get alongside. After this moment of discovery he leaves the institution and decides to train as a doctor. Patch, in his middle years and considerably older than most of the other students, glides through all of his classes and falls in love with a young woman who is also in training.

Walking around the hospitals Patch gives himself to the patients. He is in every way unconventional, playing the comic to engage patients. He is severely criticized for his approach and so sets up a house where sick and needy people can come and be cared for as people, not just patients. Patch's female companion is assisting in the 'house hospital' when a mentally challenged person walks in and is enthusiastically embraced by Patch. To cut a good, long story short, some weeks later while Patch is out, his girlfriend receives a call requesting him to visit the mentally challenged person. She goes instead and is shot and killed. Upon hearing this Patch's world is torn apart and he gives up on his 'house hospital' and also medical training.

The defining moment of the movie comes when after the funeral Patch takes a walk in the nearby woods. He comes to a cliff face and teetering over the edge, looks up to the heavens and exclaims:

"So what now? What do you want from me?"

"Yeah, I could do it," Patch continues, as he considers his options.

"We both know you wouldn't stop me," says Patch looking heavenward.

"So answer me. Tell me what you're doing," Patch pleads. He continues his lament: "Okay, let's look at the logic. You create man. Man suffers enormous amounts of pain. Man dies."

And then Patch goes on the attack. "Maybe you should have had a few more brainstorming sessions prior to creation. You rested on the seventh day, maybe you should have spent that day on compassion."

Taking a step back from the edge of the cliff, Patch tells God, "You know what, you're not worth it!"

Well meaning believers in God are quick to defend their God against Patch Adam's lament. They pull out the free will defence and argue that the death of his girlfriend was not a commentary on God but upon a misuse of the free will of humans. At this juncture however, Adams could very well retort, "But what kind of God would give such a gift [free will] that causes so much evil and suffering? Isn't this proof enough that your God is infantile and incompetent?" This, of course, is one of the points that Dostoyevsky has Ivan make in his novel about suffering.

> Imagine the reappearance of the Christ during the Spanish Inquisition of the sixteenth century. Labeled a heretic, the Son of God is brought to judgment before the cynical Grand Inquisitor, who launches a diatribe against Christ for having committed the unthinkable and unforgivable sin of giving humanity freedom of choice. This, the Inquisitor declares, is an intolerable burden, which humanity simply cannot carry.[2]

The philosopher Bayle echoes Patch Adams and Dostoyevsky's Ivan, in the *The Brothers Kazamarov*:

> There is no good mother who, having given her daughters permission to go to a dance, would not revoke that permission if she were assured that they would succumb to temptations and lose their virginity there. And any mother who, knowing for sure that this would come to pass, allowed them to go to the dance and was satisfied with exhorting them to be virtuous and with threatening to disown them if they were no longer virgins when they returned home, would, at the very least, bring upon herself the just charge that she loved neither her daughters nor chastity.[3]

The Christian might very well respond that of all the worlds that an omnipotent and omniscient God might create, this one with all its free will is the one that not only brings about more good than any other possible world but is also the kind of world where God's purposes can be brought to fruition. At this point we are jumping into deep philosophical waters which would take another book to explore. For those concerned and interested there are many good books on the subject worth exploring, but back to the heartbeat of this one.

A CHRIST–SOLDIER'S LAMENT

Sticking with the military metaphor, we might now ask how Christian soldiers might react to the above horror stories. Just as soldiers in the armed forces can begin to scream when faced with the horrors of war so too Christ-soldiers might, on facing the nightmare, feel a scream forming in their chest as they ask: "Can God really be trusted in the war zone?"

You may recall how Ruby and I with our two year old and nine month old children relocated to the heart of a Manila squatter community. Our house was a mish-mash of plywood and corrugated iron sheets. There was a knock on our door about two months after arriving. Before us was a distraught mother clutching a dying baby. We had little of the language and she spoke next to no English. What were we to do? I darted to the back of our room, grabbed my wallet and plucked some notes out of it and thrust them into the hands of the mother. The following day there were four knocks at our door. The following week, 10 knocks, and so on. Within months we had a thriving mercy ministry operation, or so I thought.

After weeks of doling out I realised it may be more appropriate to set up income generation projects so that at least these poor folk could work and pay for their own medical bills. We upped the amount invested and rather than small donations, doled out seed money for new income generation projects like setting up someone with a sewing machine, or motorbike. It still didn't seem right, even after thousands of dollars of hand-outs. It dawned on me to start up a bank. This way the poor could borrow money, set up their own businesses and then from their earnings repay the loans which in turn could be given to others. This proved very effective.

We didn't stop with the bank. We also got into infrastructure projects, medical clinics, schools, church planting and other projects. Within three and a half years we had a plethora of little businesses scattered throughout the slum. Then one day, after teaching at one of the small churches we helped plant, I came away with a gnawing impression that something was wrong with all that we had done. Ruby felt the same but neither of us could put our finger on it. We decided to ask our neighbours and no sooner had the question been put that the challenge came back; why had it taken almost four years for me to ask? I didn't feel good about where the conversation was heading but they blurted out there was indeed a major problem and the only way forward was to close down everything we had started. As agonising as it was to hear it, we were essentially told we had caused so much disharmony, misunderstanding, jealousy and relational breakdown in their community through everything we had done.

So we closed most of it down except the church. Even that emptied virtually overnight. After nigh on four years of literal blood, sweat and tears our ministry was reduced to rubble. This plunged me into a crisis of failure and then a crisis of faith.

During those four years I had prayed for nigh on three hours a day for the ministry only to see it come to naught. So what happened to my prayers? I came away from the whole episode thoroughly demoralised. What on earth can you really trust God for?

Do you remember the story of Laura, the young girl who was raped by a missionary friend of the family? Well at nineteen years of age she was also asking her pastor, Gregory Boyd, what could she really trust God for?

> When I [Gregory Boyd] asked Laura what she as a nineteen-year-old believed she was supposed to trust God for, her predictable Christian student answer was, "For God's perfect will for my life." When (to her increasing exasperation) I inquired further what that meant, she quoted one of the most quoted verses of the Bible by young Christians, Jeremiah 29:11: "For surely I know the plans I have for you, says the Lord, plans for your welfare and not for harm, to give you a future with hope." Finally, when I asked what she believed was included in the Lord's plan for her "welfare and not for harm," she exclaimed in an impatient matter-of-fact voice: "Well, to have a good marriage, of course, to have the right ministry or job and to do well in it, and to be healthy and safe. You know, just to prosper!"
>
> "Safe?" I asked. "Do you mean, to be safe from rapists?" After a long pause she nodded a sheepish yes as her eyes began to tear up.
>
> "No wonder you can't trust God, Laura," I said. "You already know that God can't be trusted to deliver on that one."

By way of conclusion, Boyd writes; "For ten years she had been encouraged by a Christian community to trust God for bodily protection when all the while she knew from personal experience that it was not only up to God to decide this matter. Intuitively, she knew that free agents like the missionary who had abused her also have a mind and will of their own. She intuitively knew that if there is no divine guarantee against little girls getting raped, there is no guarantee that nineteen-year-old women will not be raped."[6]

IS THERE ANY GOOD NEWS IN THIS GOSPEL?

In my last year at school a question began to form in my soul: Why was there so much inequality and suffering in the world? It was a question I was unable to ignore and as an irreligious person, I explained to my family that I was setting out in pursuit of truth. The next few years were filled with university, being expelled from university, drug use, drug dealing, vegetarianism and eastern mysticism, living communally and living as a hermit. I hitch-hiked with my dog 'Poet' from place to place and finally ended up in Christchurch in the South Island of New Zealand. To my utter amazement every lunch time in the main square of the city a tall black wizard would get up on a stool and keep the crowds spellbound with his incantations, interpretations and politics. While the wizard was in full flight, a short shiny-white preacher would stand on his soapbox and preach sin, hell and Jesus. These daily showdowns were too good to miss and so I became a regular at high-noon.

It was during one of these lunch times that I was approached by a Christian. He simply asked where I was staying. I informed him, "wherever - with friends or on the streets." With that he asked me to accompany him to his car. I hopped inside and within 15 minutes we pulled up outside an old concrete house. He said to follow him and so we walked down the corridor of this cold house, through the kitchen and into his bedroom. This stranger then pulled out a suitcase and proceeded to fill it with bits and pieces of his stuff. Zipping it up, he turned to me and declared, "the rest is yours as well as the room." With that, he left and there was I with a bed, a wardrobe, some clothes, a table, a side lamp and a Bible!

Who wouldn't at least attempt to read this book after such a demonstration of love? Never before had I owned a personal Bible. It proved to be dynamite, and quite simply blew my life away. While in the hippie drug counter-culture, I blamed the world's woes on the 'system'. But taking the step to read the Bible introduced me to another cause: mini-me! The Bible was absolutely clear about structural and systemic evil but was also forthright in declaring my sin sickness. I read how at birth[7] a foreign virus had invaded my body and self. It then attacked and attached itself to every part of who I was and proceeded to transform these parts into weapons that I would use against other people.[8] To put it crudely, these biblical missiles nuked me. These revelations devastated me and wreaked havoc in my inner most being. All my tall and lofty thoughts about myself came tumbling down. I now had to acknowledge the truth about myself.

This was made easier by another equally demanding discovery. I saw Jesus in the pages of the Bible. He wasn't the Jesus I expected. He didn't come across as the steely-eyed fundamentalist, screaming from a soapbox pulpit. Nor did he resemble the vacant-eyed overly effeminate mystic type often characterized in 'Jesus' movies.[9] Rather, I saw a divine human being of obvious deep emotion who cared about the things we care about. I could relate to this Jesus. But what especially appealed, was his rebellious streak. This Jesus mixed it with those considered 'bad company' by the elite of his day; with the underclass, the social casualties, the widows, orphans, unemployed, sick and deviants. He was often with those deemed rude, untutored and unlettered; hated and scorned by others. In a daring and delightful way, the Jesus I read about – always seemed to be with the wrong people at the wrong time in the wrong places. I warmed to him and wanted to join his merry band.

However there were a few sharp edges to this Jesus as well. Most of the disciples had altercations with him. It would not be easy being his follower, but surely I thought, it must be easier than following my twisted and tortured self. The hard sayings of Jesus scared me. For nine months I walked the park, wrestling with myself over whether I would make that commitment. Even then, I could see clearly the call to Christ was not just about receiving a new life, but giving away my own. This could not be entered into lightly. Having concluded there was no other way to live, on Easter Monday morning in 1976, in the cold, barren house in Christchurch, I knelt down and pledged my life to Jesus. As I stepped outside that room and began walking down the corridor I sensed I had begun a new life as a new person.

At the outset I was very clear on one thing. If this gospel cost Jesus his life then this same gospel would also cost me dearly. I was reminded by Boyd that the good news of the gospel is NOT that we will never suffer, get raped, be maimed or die an early death. If as Christ-soldiers, we seek to overthrow evil wherever it is found and in its place establish the Kingdom of God, then suffering will be our constant companion. Jesus suffered and told us to expect suffering,[10] Paul and the early apostles suffered and challenged us to follow in their footsteps.[11] Suffering is never an intention but it is a consequence. Going to difficult places of discipleship and seeking justice for all will put us in harm's way. In this war zone, Christ-soldiers will be persecuted, suffer famine, be assailed by demonic forces and get caught in the crossfire. Children will be abducted, women violently raped, and even little children at the age of nine will not be spared. What then can we expect from God? Both Jesus and Paul were clear on at least one thing – suffering. But surely there is more? Surely in the midst of suffering God can be trusted for something more?

THINGS THAT SURVIVE THE WAR ZONE

The Apostle Paul framed his existence as a war time one. He talked of being in a fight and of waging war[12] and so not surprisingly, evil stalked him and he suffered as a soldier. Bad things happened to Paul. He took his hits and at times was a casualty. He endured troubles, hardships, distresses, beatings, imprisonments, riots, hard work, sleepless nights, and hunger.[13] These were his dark forest moments in the war zone. In the heat of the battle Paul turned to his God for healing and protection, but he often bumped into the God of Sally, Laura, Greta and countless others; a God who doesn't always heal or protect. In Lystra, for example, Paul was laid out cold by a good stoning. A violent crowd turned on him and threw *real* rocks at him. He must have ended up a bloody mess, for the crowd thought he was dead and left him.[14] Again where was the God who promised protection for his children? Another time, Paul believed it was right for him to go to Spain but his attempts turned to custard. Satan, Paul argued, stopped him.[15] Where then, was the triumphant Christ who had overcome the evil one? Then Paul came down with a niggling, distressing physical complaint but after praying for healing, came to the conclusion that this sickness was here to stay.[16] Where then, was the promise of healing? Then at other times Paul saw victory with the promises of God fulfilled in amazing ways. But protection, provision and healing are *not always* guaranteed. So then, what are the absolute guarantees in the war zone?

Paul was convinced of one thing, that in the war zone with all its hardships, danger, and demons,[17] nothing can ever separate us from God's love. Further, Matthew and other biblical writers remind us of another sure thing: Heaven![18] In the midst of all the mayhem and madness of the war we can trust that God loves us and wants us to inherit heaven. In terms of absolute guarantees for all believers, anywhere at any time, that seems to be it. Of course, wrapped round his love are such treasures as forgiveness, the fruit of the Spirit and fellowship with God.

I would like to think that I have arrived at a place where this is enough. In the heat of the battle, in the trenches of ministry, in the crossfire and flak from both sides, I am to be content with God's love and heaven. That is not to say, I don't pray for so much more. I do! I pray for protection, deliverance, healing and victory. I have learned however, these are sometimes given but not always guaranteed. What I fear is that for many of us, being loved by God and going to heaven are simply not enough. We want more and are deeply disappointed when God doesn't deliver. Sooner or later huge disappointments will come our way. To pray during those excruciating times is absolutely the right thing to do. To believe that God will somehow make a difference is so important. But it is also a disturbing reality that God will not always come through for us. Why this is so is the subject matter of the next chapter. Suffice to say here by way of conclusion that we must settle in our hearts that we do not have a God in heaven who will always protect us from harm's way nor will he always make life sweet and happy for us. That is not in his job description. God does however guarantee the two aforementioned realities; his love and heaven. The question is, are we content enough with these? It has been my observation that those Christians who are not content with these and want so much more, usually turn on God and charge him with callous indifference when life inevitably becomes unfair or cruel. These dear folk are but a short step away from baling out and giving themselves over to being an ex-believer. If only someone had got to them right at the outset and helped them to see that in a war zone we must have realistic expectations of life and God. Even though they may have felt God was not there for them when things really happened, my contention is that God was there for them, he was there in love and for eternity. For consumers these will never be enough, but for Christ's soldiers they will be everything. This is the place we have to get to if we are to stand fast in the struggle against evil.

1. Gregory A. Boyd, *Satan and the Problem of Evil: Constructing a Trinitarian Warfare Theodicy* (IVP, 2001), pp.158–9.
2. This is taken from Dostoyevsky's novel *The Brothers Kazamarov*. Another novel that captures the issue of evil is *The Plague* by Camus.
3. Pierre Bayle, *Historical and Critical Dictionary*. Selections translated with an introduction and notes by Richard Popkin. (Bobbs-Merrill, 1965), 177–178.
4. At a popular level Philip Yancey has written much about issues of disappointment, pain and God. At a theological level Alister McGrath is worth a read as is Gregory Boyd. The latter for example has a book entitled, *Is God to Blame?* At a philosophical level, I recommend William Lane Craig and Alvin Plantinga. Their books are hard going but worth the chew! A most comprehensive 'non-christian' attempt at the problem of evil, and again from an in-depth philosophical level is that of Susan Neiman's *Evil in Modern Thought* (Melbourne: Scribe Publishing, 2002).
5. Gregory A. Boyd, *Satan and the Problem of Evil: Constructing a Trinitarian Warfare Theodicy* (IVP, 2001), pp.158–9.
6. Gregory A. Boyd, p.158–9.
7. Psalm 51:5
8. This and other descriptions of sin can be found in Cornelius Plantinga's *Not the Way It's Supposed to Be: A Breviary of Sin* (Apollos, 1995).
9. A notable exemption being the 2004 release of *The Passion*, directed by Mel Gibson.
10. Matthew 5:11,44; 16:24–25; Luke 12:53; 21:12; John 15:20, 21:18–19
11. Hebrews 12:3; James 5:10; 1 Peter 2:20–21
12. Ephesians 6:12; 2 Corinthians 10:3–4.
13. 2 Corinthians 6:3–10.
14. Romans 14:8–20.
15. 1 Thessalonians 2:17–18.
16. 2 Corinthians 12:7–9.
17. Romans 8:35, 38.
18. Matthew 6:19–20.

CHAPTER FOUR

PRAYER AS A WEAPON

I begin writing this chapter in Melbourne, Australia. I am here speaking at a conference and staying with friends. As I am a naturally early riser I have already spent time in prayer, meditated on the scriptures, read a chapter of a book on Dietrich Bonhoeffer, the German Pastor who stood up to Hitler, showered and had breakfast. It is still only 7.30am. Tired of waiting for my friends to wake into the world, I head for the nearest café to keep to the one hour one page per day writing regime.

So here I am, in one of my favourite places, a café. What a way to begin the day! Not two tables away sits a man in his 50s, he is alone and talking away to someone who isn't there. He turns his head, nods, waves his hands, points and raises his voice. To the observer, he is alone. I am reminded of the excellent movie *A Beautiful Mind* (2001) about John Nash (Russell Crowe), the Nobel Prize winner of mathematics. The movie plots Nash's slow but sure descent into the world of schizophrenia. He ends up living his life around three companions whom he sincerely believes exist. He walks talks and plays with them. But to the outsider, there is only Nash behaving very strangely.

These are the people you encounter in the war zone. The battlefields are strewn with them, outcasts, victims; the weak, the broken and discarded who no longer fit comfortably into our cruel and chaotic world. Jesus bumped into them all the time. A boy traumatized by convulsions, a woman bent over at the waist, a maniac in a cemetery. We, too, should be disturbed by these tortured souls. When encountering these damaged humans Jesus often looked up and prayed to his Father in heaven. We are invited to do likewise. But herein lies the rub. How do you pray for these complex characters? What do you pray? When and where do you pray? Do you pray?

I remember being asked by some neighbours of ours in the slums of Manila to come with them to the hospital to pray for their uncle who had just died. My initial understanding was that I was to pray a sort of dedication prayer but upon entering the room I was asked to pray that he might come back to life again! I recalled Jesus and even Paul had done this sort of thing. But could I? How do you pray in the war zone? Ruby was also asked to pray for another neighbour. From the waist up she was a beautiful Filipino but from the waist down she was abnormally huge and extremely sick. She was suffering from kidney failure. How do you pray? In New Zealand, when I was a pastor of a church in Auckland, I got a phone call from complete strangers asking if I could come to their place and pray through each room in their flat. The students informed me objects would move of their own accord along with other bizarre and strange happenings. I felt very much like one of the Ghostbusters, but upon arriving wondered how on earth to pray about such things?

Prayer, it would seem, is very difficult with strange people. Not surprisingly, many a Christian social worker settles for things that are more straightforward, perhaps sitting with people, providing food and shelter, assisting in advocacy or caring through counselling. In all of this good activity there is often little if any prayer. Why is it that the practice of prayer, the very activity that makes Christians unique from other social work providers, is often the thing we shy away from? Richard Lovelace writes, "most of those who are praying are not praying about social issues and most of those who are active in social issues are not praying very much."[1]

Sally, the young follower of Jesus who was snatched at a party by a gang, prayed for protection but God didn't come through for her. The prayers of Greta's parents didn't stop her being kidnapped and killed. God didn't spare Laura from the trauma of being raped by a missionary friend of the family. These sorts of stories, certainly in the eyes of the world, make prayer more like a lottery and those who persist in it a source of amusement.

THE SEA OF AMBIGUITY

My first degree was in sociology, and in one of the earliest assignments I learned the definition of a sociologist. This is the type of person who goes to a football game and instead of watching the game is busy watching the crowd. Unfortunately this is so true of me. When I go to the mall with Ruby she is forever telling me to stop looking at the people. Wherever I am, I can't help but scan the crowds and try and see patterns. When I walk into a church for the first time my little antennae are up trying to discern what is really happening. A key word in sociology is 'variables'. In any given situation there may be a number of variables at work which are the causal factors in a situation. It gets interesting when you have to try and work out which variables actually influence other variables. Without boring you further, when it comes to praying in the war zone we need to appreciate that there are a number of variables at work. Where it gets tricky is that in some contexts one variable will be more influential than another. Praying in the war zone is not as straightforward as we may like it to be. It demands an appreciation of the variables and then a discernment to know which variables are at play. Each of the following variables may have a bearing on whether prayers will be answered in the war zone.

I am again indebted to Gregory Boyd for the following list to which I have added my own interpretation and stories.

1. God's will – (1 John 5:14, James 4:3). God's will was clearly revealed in Christ, for example, healing the sick and setting free the captives. We are to do likewise. If only it was as straightforward as that. God's 'will' may be clear to him but in our sick and sorry world he is at times unable to achieve his ideal will. Paul suffered from some sort of complaint (2 Corinthians 12:7–10). You would have thought God's ideal will would have been to heal but due to Paul's human propensity to pride, grace to endure rather than outright healing was granted. As Boyd writes, "God it seems works toward the greatest good achievable in a nonideal situation."[2]

2. The faith of the person being prayed for – (Mark 6:5–6, Matthew 9:22; cf. Luke 7:50; 17:19). At times Jesus was quick to say a person was healed because of their faith. I remember when I first went to a healing meeting, the American Pastor John Wimber of Vineyard fame was speaking and asked the Holy Spirit to come on the meeting. It was absolutely amazing what transpired. Some people shook, others fell, some laughed and laughed, others were set free from demons and you name it. That night I witnessed a dimension of God's Power that seemed gentle, genuine and very attractive. The following week I gave myself to prayer and fasting and after two days had the distinct conviction I had a problem with unbelief or more specifically, selective believing. I could believe God for forgiveness but not for the filling of the Spirit. I could trust God for help but not for healing. I sensed I had to confess this sin of unbelief. A few days later while enjoying a bath a little bubble went off – inside of me. It was like a surge of ecstatic joy. A few hours later at the dinner table, more bubbles in quick succession exploded to the point that I had to excuse myself from the table and dart off to the bedroom. No sooner had I closed the door than I dropped to the ground and laughed and laughed for the next two hours. The presence of God around and in me was so intense my reflex reaction was one of hilarity. In this instance, my faith was needful.

Unfortunately, some well meaning folk within the Church have taken this one variable and made it into *the* variable. "Your faith" is now set up as the pre-condition or pre-requisite for everything. If a person is not filled with the Spirit or healed then it is because they lack faith. My story is simply to remind us that our faith is a part in the puzzle.

3. The faith of people praying for others – (Luke 5:20, Matthew 8:13). Our faith must not be set up as the formula or key determining factor. One day, I was walking down an alley in the slums where we lived and was suddenly approached by a distraught man. He asked me to come to his place and pray for his brother. I asked why he needed prayer. I was told that his brother delighted in bathing in the creek that was situated nearby, which was essentially a urine and faeces infested waterway. I was informed the man had tried more than once to drive nails through his hands. Who could not to pray for such a tortured person? I entered the home and asked the man if I could pray for him. No sooner had I started praying then he dropped to the floor. I waited for him to recover and prayed again. He once more fell to the floor. On the third time I sat him in a chair, prayed and again he hit the floor. I began to suspect demonic activity. As he was lying on the ground all I could see was the white of his eyes. With this I thought, "Oh, no!"

I then spoke in English and asked what the names of the demons were. In English, three names came back. The man didn't speak English! Interestingly, they were religious spirits which may explain the 'nails in the hands' episode. For the next hour or so we prayed without success. I returned home and realized my faith level for this sort of thing wasn't that high. So for the next week I prayed, fasted and read and re-read books on demon possession. I then asked a Filipino pastor to accompany me hoping that his faith would suffice if mine wavered again. This time, quietness seemed to come over the man and the last time I heard about him he was happily married with children and in work. The variable here was not his faith but mine and that of my Filipino pastor friend.

4. Persistence in prayer – (Luke 11:5–8; 18:1–8, 1 Thessalonians 5:17). Boyd writes, "some rocks can be lifted in a minute, but others take hours. So it is in prayer."[3] There is a laboring dimension to prayer, not to try and twist the arm of a reluctant God, but rather to keep praying in utter desperation. One of my favorite popular writers and speakers is John Ortberg. In his very popular book *Walking on the Water* he encourages the spiritual discipline of praying for the one thing every day for six months. To reinforce this discipline, he tells the story of Doug and Bob.[4] The latter, a new Christian chanced upon Jesus' promise, "ask whatever you will in my name and you shall receive it." With this in mind, Bob declared to Doug that he would pray for Africa to which Doug encouraged Bob to narrow it down a bit and so Kenya was decided upon as the target. Everyday Bob persisted in praying but months later nothing seemed to eventuate. Then one night whilst at a dinner function he met a Kenyan woman who ran an orphanage there. They got talking and she ended up inviting him to her country. The visit shocked him. He came face to face with flesh and blood in absolute poverty. On his return to America he wrote to some of the large pharmaceutical companies imploring them to no longer throw away their surplus drugs but to gift them to orphanages like the one he had visited in Kenya. All the while Bob continued to pray daily. The orphanage received box loads of drugs and invited

Bob back for a celebration to which the President of Kenya was also invited. Bob and the President got talking and Bob advised the President to set the political prisoners free in his land. The President did so, and when it came to selecting a new Cabinet the President of Kenya rang Bob asking for his advice. All this after six months of persistent labouring prayer.

5. The number of people praying – (Nehemiah 9:1; 2 Chronicles 7:14; Matthew 26:36, 41; Acts 1:13–14; Ephesians 6:19–20; James 5:13–16). Boyd writes, "the bigger the rock, the more likely it is you'll need help lifting it. There is no reason to think that the labour of prayer is any different."[5] For the first four years of our sojourn in the slums of Manila I got horrendously sick. The female mosquitoes of Manila gave me dengue three times but it was a dose of amoebic dysentery that I remember the most. Quite literally, I was passing blood and vomiting often with both ends going at the same time. Ruby had prayed but to no avail. Our team time was scheduled for that week and prior to departing she said, "If you're still sick when I get back you're going to hospital." To be honest, I was most reluctant to escape to a hospital because when the poor get sick this option is often not open to them. This was all part of our seeking to participate and identify as far as we could. But in this instance, I knew Ruby was right. Then quite miraculously I suddenly stopped running to the bucket and the toilet. When Ruby returned we discovered that the end to my agonies had come at the very time the team (consisting of 20 adults) had prayed as one for my healing. What Ruby could not pray alone others could together.

6. Human free will – (Luke 7:30). God's purposes can be thwarted by free will agents. God's will, does not simply override free will. Boyd counsels: "Prayer affects everything, but it may not have the outcome we are praying for; it is persuasive, not coercive. People still make free choices."[6] In Christmas 2003 I was walking down the main street of our city and noticed someone familiar passing by. My immediate reflex action was to point a finger and say to the person, "I know you." He clicked straight away and said, "Hi Michael." The guy had been a missionary – a one hundred and ten percenter. Today he is a confessed non-follower and Jesus is just another swear word. I enjoy this guy, especially his sense of humor, but I deeply grieve over his decision. I pray for him but have to admit that my prayers are not magic bullets that will turn him back to faith. Nor is my God the kind who will stomp over his free will in response to my prayers.

God plays by the rules, especially the rules he in his wisdom chose for this world. One of those rules is for human's freedom to choose. He is a God of restraint. The American writer Philip Yancey best describes this divine shyness in God when he writes;

> Soren Kierkegaard wrote about God's light touch: "Omnipotence which can lay its hand so heavily upon the world can also make its touch so light that the

creature receives independence." Sometimes, I concede, I wish that God used a heavier touch. My faith suffers from too much freedom, too many temptations to disbelieve. At times I want God to overwhelm me, to overcome my doubts with certainty, to give final proofs of his existence and his concern. I want God to take a more active role in my personal history too. I want quick and spectacular answers to my prayers, healing for my diseases, protection and safety for my loved ones. I want a God without ambiguity, One to whom I can point for the sake of my doubting friends. When I think these thoughts, I recognize in myself a thin, hollow echo of the challenge that Satan hurled at Jesus two thousand years ago. God resists those temptations now as Jesus resisted them on earth, settling instead for a slower, gentler way.[7]

When you survey the picture of Jesus in the Gospels there is not a hint that he ever employed manipulative techniques to get what he wanted. There was no twisting of an arm, no overly coercive action. This Jesus, the Son of the living God, self-limits himself out of respect for human freedom.

7. Angelic free will – (Daniel 10:12–13; 1 Thessalonians 2:17–18). Both of these scriptures refer to instances when either prayers (Daniel) or plans (Paul) were thwarted by Satan. We can infer from the text that both cases were in tune with God's will but the opposition was such that it could not be carried out at that time. Walter Wink writes, "Principalities and Powers are able to hold the Lord at bay…prayer involves not just God and people, but God and people and the Powers. What God is able to do in the world is hindered, to a considerable extent, by the rebelliousness, resistance, and self-interest of the Powers exercising their freedom under God."[8]

I was speaking to a group of about a hundred Christian youth workers training in community development. When I suggested that at times Satan and his forces act outside of and against God's will they were very quick to refer to the Book of Job and point out that Satan had to get God's permission to act against Job and his family. That free will 'good angels' chose to rebel against God and side with the evil forces of darkness was not up for dispute. However the students did dispute that these same angels could still act independent of God. For a more detailed debate on Job please refer to the footnote below,[9] but suffice to say here that Scripture does seem to suggest two situations. There are those instances when Satan acts with God's permission and other times when Satan seems to act of his own accord. If this is so, then our theology should include both. Robert Alden, for example, writes; "that at times his [Satan] power seems not only supernatural but also a threat to God's sovereign and beneficent control of the world – at other times the Satan seems like a vain, weak, and hopeless antagonist against the omnipotent God of the universe."[10] Being a thinking disciple is not always easy. It seems to me that we must have the cerebral capacity to hold seemingly opposite or contradictory things in critical tension with each other.

Where some get into theological trouble, is when they see a few instances of how God or Satan operate and then argue that is the way that God or Satan always operates. A better theology is to argue that God is all powerful without equal but that this same God has a genuine opponent in Satan where the latter at times wins a battle but has already lost the war.

8. The presence of sin – (Joshua 7:10–11; Mark 11:25; James 5:16). Achan faced the famed walls of Jericho. Archaeology has it that there were actually two high walls surrounding the city with some fourteen feet between them. The odds were decidedly against Joshua, Achan and the rabble of Israel ever taking this fortified city. But they were learning to attend to the words of Yahweh and as strange as it may seem God called for a close relative of the 'Mexican Wave' to bring the walls of Jericho tumbling down. Encircling their opponents, they shouted in unison, smashing the walls and stunning the people into defeat.

Next scene we read of the Israelites being defeated by a far smaller town and thirty six of their number die in the skirmish. Joshua struggles to accept this defeat after their demolition job on Jericho. He withdraws to the quiet to give ear to his God who is quick to inform that one of their number took some stuff from Jericho that wasn't supposed to be even touched. To cut a long story short, Achan is spotted, singled out and sent to the front of the class whereupon he confesses his crime. He appropriated for himself approximately 2kg of silver and some label 'gear' (clothing) from Babylonia. Despite the apparent small size of the booty, Achan was stoned to death in the Valley of Trouble, along with his entire family. I don't know about you, but if I was one of the Israelites on the day of that stoning, I'd walk away troubled by one overwhelming question, did the punishment fit the crime?

All Achan took was 2kg of silver and a few choice items of clothing and for that his life was taken from him. Robert Clinton gives us a clue to comprehending these puzzling passages. The issues were never about clothing but learning obedience – even in the very small things. What was at stake here is what Clinton calls an *obedience check:*,

> An *obedience check* is a process item through which a person learns to recognize, understand and obey God's voice. The person encounters this early in his or her development and repeatedly throughout life. Through it God tests a person's personal response to revealed truth....It is one thing to obey when it seems logical and necessary, but it is quite another when the obedience calls for something that doesn't make sense. Obedience doesn't always hinge on understanding. It did not make sense ethically or practically to kill Isaac, yet Abraham obeyed...Would Abraham remain loyal to God and believe in Him when the pressure was on? These tests revealed that faith and loyalty to God were a part of Abraham's character.[11]

On the comparatively big–time stuff; shouting at Jericho, Achan passed the hearing test. He heard God and acted appropriately. On the smaller stuff, Achan proved hard of hearing. He, along with the rabble of Israel, had been explicitly warned not to snatch stuff, however small, from the rubble of Jericho.[12] A damaging consequence of Achan's actions was that God could not do what he had done before. Human sin tied his hands. In this instance God was limited by human disobedience. The opposite is equally true when James tells us the prayer of a righteous person avails much. What God can and cannot do sometimes hinges on human behaviour.

CONCLUSION

At one stage we converted our toilet into a chat room. People could come in, sit down and reflect and then write their musings on the wall. One day, my youngest wrote, "If God can do anything, even the impossible, then…" This is a prevailing view: God can do the impossible, he can do anything. And even though I agree with the spirit of these statements, this does not mean God will do that which is inconsistent or illogical. For example, he will not turn black into white just for the fun of it, nor will he try and make two plus two equal six. God will not act against what he has already set in place, namely a divine respect for freedom. God works within what he has created. God is truly incarnational in that he works within certain realities. The variables form a reality God has chosen to limit himself to. In light of these variables, according to Boyd, "God genuinely faces in every particular situation a reality distinct from himself that has some say-so over and against himself…God has restricted the exercise of his own omnipotence."[13] When praying amongst the ruins and for the ruined, we must be aware of this reality that has say-so over and against God. This is not to belittle God but to locate God in a complex world. Prayer is not as straightforward as we might want or need it to be. But for a prayer warrior in the war zone, these variables are no obstacle. Prayer warriors are marked by a 'whatever it takes' spirit. They will work within these realities, adjust and adapt, and stay on their knees for the sake of others.

CHAPTER FIVE

ORDER OUT OF CHAOS

The nightmares of the war zone can have a disturbing affect on our prayer life. We live in a complex world where there are many variables at play which can influence the outcomes of prayer. We continue examining the motive of prayer by exploring another reason why some soldiers abandon the weapon of prayer in the heat of battle. It often has to do with the theological diet being served up in many churches and colleges. We are being asked to swallow the idea that God has already decided what he is going to do and if this is the case then, it is reasonable to ask: Why pray? The pat answer is that prayer is good for us; it exerts a positive influence on the one praying. Implicit in this response is that nothing of note really hinges on our prayer life. If the future is a done deal in God's mind, then it could be argued there is little point to prayer. But is the future foreordained and predetermined? Does God really know all of the future? These are not easy questions.

THE 'SETTLED' FUTURE

In the Bible there are a number of accounts where God pulled back the curtains on the future and allowed his servants to see what was about to transpire. The prophet Ezekiel was told one morning that his wife would die later that day.[1] Isaiah, at the very outset of his ministry as a communicator was told that in the future few would listen to him or heed his warnings.[2] Joseph at 17 years of age was told in a dream, that one day his older brothers would bow down to him.[3] God told Paul in the midst of a violent storm that no lives would be lost but that the ship would be wrecked on an island.[4] Abraham was told one day his name would be great.[5] All of these predictions came true. In Abraham's case, his name is today revered by almost half the world's population, by Christians, Jews and Muslims.

Jesus also had this remarkable ability to predict the future, even down to specific details. Within the space of 15 verses (Mark 14), Mark has Jesus predicting five future events. The disciples will meet a man carrying a jar of water; this person will then direct them to a certain location and one of the disciples will betray him. All came to pass. The odds one of the disciples might double-cross Jesus were always on, but actually naming the one who will do the deed is truly predictive. Further Jesus says all the disciples would flee from him in his hour of crisis. And finally, that Peter would disown him. Again, the odds on Peter shying away from admitting he was a Jesus follower were always going to be good given his personality. But that Jesus predicted this would happen after a certain rooster crowed twice is beyond coincidence.

It is clear God knew what was about to happen in the war zone, and informed his people beforehand. Has this ever happened to you? I will never forget the duty free radio and tape recorder I bought on the way to Manila. While in the slums it proved to be a life-saver. On Saturdays I could get the cricket from Australia and most nights found me tuning in to the BBC news. The radio was kept on a shelf just above where I prayed. One night during prayer I had a distinct 'impression' that I was to take the radio off the shelf and place it on the table in front of me. What was implicit in this 'impression' was that someone would try and steal the radio that night. In the morning there was a gaping hole in the wall next to the shelf. Someone had pulled back a piece of plywood believing the radio would be in its normal place. God however, had got there first. He had seemingly peeled back the future.

In reflecting on another illustration from one of the most devastating and depressing seasons of my life I can also see the almighty hand at work. Back in New Zealand fresh from Manila I was grieving for the life I had left behind. I had been hurt by some of my colleagues, and in my pain blurted out, "I resign." This rush of the blood to the head had come after some rigorous debates about important philosophical directions in our ministry. But in hindsight it may have been better if I had hit the pause button and asked for a leave of absence. Instead, like a child in a sand pit, I picked up my toys and stormed off. I felt I had made a horrendous mistake in leaving the Philippines when we did. I have since come to see that if you leave something with a right attitude another door invariably opens up, however if you depart in a way that dishonours God or people, the next step is often in to a wilderness time. Most evenings in my wilderness time found me sitting alone in a dark corner of the bedroom buckled over in gut wrenching tears with no new ministry options opening up anywhere. About six months into this desert I got impatient, believing I had done 'my time'. I made my protest known to God and no sooner had I done so than a small snapshot of a picture suddenly lit up in the imagination chamber of my heart. All I saw was a small black handkerchief falling to the ground. My heavenly Counsellor whispered from on high that no new door of service would open until I recovered from the necessary grieving stage of leaving Manila. That one small seed thought whispered into my present prepared me for the future that God knew I would have. I patiently sat out another 18 months.

A year later the handkerchief dropped closer to the ground and a call came to consider being a pastor at an inner-city church in the heart of Melbourne, Australia. The night before we were about to fly out I had a vivid dream. In it I was speaking to the church and small fires began to break out all around the walls of the building. These were not fires of renewal but of fiery criticism. As the fires ignited I heard a voice urging me to continue speaking the truth. Next morning I shook off the dream and headed for the airport. Sure enough within the next nine months I found myself battling all sorts of issues and criticisms which came to a head with a challenge to an elder in the church who was a practicing homosexual. As stated, I am not homophobic, nor did I have a problem with a person of homosexual orientation being in leadership. The issue was that rather than being abstinent, he was actively practising. I was asked to accommodate this and other unscriptural practices but in all good conscience I could not. I was asked to resign. From the outset to the bitter end I continued to speak the truth as I saw it, out of faithfulness to God and the dream he had given me.

There is it seems *Someone* at the very centre of the Universe who knows us and our future. If this is the case then the smartest thing to do is to spend as much time as possible in prayer. When we spend quality time with the God who knows our future, we create spaces where he can come to us in the present and prepare us for the future he knows we will have to face. He may whisper words or short sentences into our spirits. He may deposit dreams into our sleep state or drop video-like streams into our imagination. In these supernatural 'epiphany like' experiences God is giving us insights into the future.

Have you ever had an experience, in the shower or other private place, when suddenly a thought just pops into your consciousness? You may be driving to work when unexpectedly an idea moves into your mind, or walking along the beach and find a new sentence gatecrashing your meditation? You ask, "Where on earth did that come from?" This is what happened to me when I received the picture of the handkerchief and the dream about the fires. These whispers into my soul occurred in such a memorable way as to prepare me for what lay ahead.

Brother Yun, a Chinese Pastor who was imprisoned and then forced to flee China because of his faith; recounts the numerous times the Lord gave him dreams and warnings about the future. In his remarkable book, he relates one incident that occurred when he was about to get his family out of Myanmar (Burma) and relocate to Germany. He had a vivid dream two nights before leaving in which his son passed through customs and crossed the border into Thailand safely. He was detained. Sure enough that's exactly how it happened. The Burmese authorities, thinking he was a spy, had him imprisoned in Yangon City. In this facility that housed 10,000 men he was allowed a two minute shower once every four days. Yun writes, "no words can adequately describe the conditions there. Many of the prisoners suffered from AIDS, and a large number had leprosy. The smell of rotting flesh invaded every corner of the dark, forsaken facility, where precious souls are left to die in silence."[6] For no reason at all, this follower of Jesus was sentenced to seven years in a hell hole. While in prison a plague swept through the place and eventually struck Brother Yun. Parasites invaded his body and worms crawled under his skin. At one point he was rendered unconscious by the disease and had to be taken to the prison hospital. While in prison he saw a number of people come to Jesus for the first time. Soon after his sentence, Yun received a whisper in his spirit. He was told by God that in seven months he would be released. True to that promise, on September 18, 2001 Brother Yun was taken from the prison and assisted onto a plane bound for Germany where his wife and children were desperately waiting.

These examples speak of a God who sows seeds in the present that have the potential to prepare us for the future. These seeds are multiform: dreams, seed-thought invasions, audible voices, visions, pictures, impressions, heaven-sent urges, angelic messengers or divinely sent people, prophecies, quickened passages of Scripture, coincidences and incidences – you name it. However, none of these should stand alone as guides or sources of truth, right or wrong they need to be explored carefully, evaluated by trusted friends and examined in light of Scripture. Regardless, I fear that dreams, prophecies, seed thoughts and God-given inspirations, along with prayer are not being allowed the important place in our lives that they deserve. Even in the war zone, it is often the case that these seeds and whispers come in to us through the intimacy of prayer.

The saddest truth on the planet is that few Christians spend intimate, quality time with the One they have made their deepest promises to. The best most can offer up is about five minutes before they jump into a morning shower or as they lie in bed late at night. Relating to God on the run or in a time squeeze is hardly conducive to prepare us for life in the war zone.

All the biblical heroes came into the presence of God on a regular basis. In our household I am always the first up and during winter, I either strike a match and light a fire or turn on the heater. Soon after I strike another match and light up my relationship with Jesus. I am the sort of person who needs to tune into Jesus at least once, if not three times every 24 hours. I am absolutely clear about what it means to be a prayer warrior. While I would never insist on people doing what I do, I can recommend what being a prayer warrior will do in your life. Jesus made it a regular practice to withdraw to have quiet, intimate quality time with his father. In the war zone, this was a must to prepare him for what was ahead.

PHILOSOPHICAL TSUNAMIS

This notion of God knowing the future is not without its problems. Implicit is the idea that if he can predict the future then he must also know about the suffering and afflictions coming our way. While God knows what is to happen, he doesn't necessarily cause it. But still, why does he allow it? What kind of God would allow a Hitler to rise knowing he would kill six million Jews? Why would an all-knowing God allow a Sally to be brutalized? What kind of God would allow earthquakes, floods, fires, and the forces of nature to wreak such havoc? And what kind of God would allow my first 25 years of service to be such a struggle?

During the Monsoon season our slum was continually drenched in rain causing minor floods. Typhoons often transformed this poorest of make-shift villages into a 20 foot high septic tank. The nearby river would burst its banks and within minutes filthy rat, snake and disease infested waters would rise. At times I plunged into these waters on an inflated tyre tube to do the rounds and see if anyone needed to be plucked from the toxic tide. To say the least, these 'pastoral visits' were reminders, as if I needed any further evidence, of how cruel 'Mother Nature' can be. The waters swept away what little people had, devastated their slum with more sickness and demoralized their spirits. After the tenth or twentieth typhoon it was ludicrous to talk about how these disasters fitted into some grand heavenly scheme. Far from these crucibles of harsh circumstance polishing character in people, they invariably dampened hope, courage and love. These wet seasons extinguished sparks of resilience and initiative adding more misery than good. Despite what we might like to believe, very little good came from them.

All of us were graphically reminded of such cruel realities when the killer wave struck much of Asia the day after Christmas 2004. Tourist spots in Thailand became massive graveyards, and tens upon thousands of the dead were little boys and girls washed away whilst eating breakfast or innocently playing. The Indian Ocean became a sea of sorrow. Christian apologists and evangelists rightly call people to see the amazing order in creation but in this tsunami we saw chaos and disorder. We are rightly told of the beauty of nature, but here the natural world showed its brutal side. Science has helped unearth the many functions of nature but there was something awfully dysfunctional in the way the Indian plate and the Burma plate of the earth's crust began to grind together with the resulting stress of one pulling down on the other, causing a massive displacement of water in the Indian Ocean. On Christmas Day nature cooperated with humans staging a beautiful sunny day, the day after she turned on humanity and in a single wave destroyed over five million homes. "Nature does not abhor evil," writes Howard Bloom, "she embraces it…. Death, destruction, and fury do not disturb the Mother of our world; they are merely parts of her plan."[7]

Annie Dillard writes, "The universe that suckled us is a monster.... A robot programmed to kill."[8]

Did God know about *this* tsunami?[9] And if he did, when did he know? Classic theism argues that God knew from eternity and therefore allowed it to happen. For some Christians, this is too much to ask. In their reaction, they have re-examined scripture and re-thought their theology and philosophy to see if God's foreknowledge needs to be re-defined. As a result, some Christians now believe that God fully knows the past and present but not all of the future. In other words, prior to Boxing Day, God knew all about previous tsunamis and the terrible devastation they wreak in peoples' lives and knew future tsunamis were possible but did not necessarily know *this* tsunami was going to happen. Further, God was fully cognizant of all factors when on Boxing Day the Indian and Burma plates ground together and what the resulting wave was doing to countless innocent people. So God knew the past and the present, but like all of us, God was surprised by *this* tsunami. This school of thought has become known as Open Theism and as this book is about God and suffering it deserves attention.

THE 'OPEN' FUTURE

Traditional and open theism both state that God perfectly knows but differ on the content of what he knows. One says that God exhaustively knows all (past, present and future) and even knows what will transpire in our lives. The open theists believe that what God knows he knows perfectly, but that he does not entirely know the future. There are, in other words, some open spaces. How they are filled and what will happen, even intrigues God. In other words, 'stuff happens' in the war zone that even God did not have foreknowledge of.

Open theists point to God's genuine regret over the wickedness of his creation. What his free will agents ended up doing to each other "grieved him to his heart."[10] How then do you explain that regret if God knew about it all before it happened? Gregory Boyd paints the problem like this:

> Now, if everything about world history were exhaustively settled and known by God as such before he created the world, God would have known with absolute certainty that humans would come to this wicked state, at just this time, before he created them. But how then, could he authentically regret having made humankind? Doesn't the fact that God regretted the way things turned out – to

the point of starting over – suggest that it wasn't a foregone conclusion at the time God created human beings that they would fall into this state of wickedness?[11]

Again, take for example the case of Saul we discussed in chapter one. His daughter Michal married the young David and Saul proved to be a father-in-law from hell. Not content with hurling insults at David he reverted to throwing spears. A radical evil inhabited his soul such that he put many in harm's way. In the end, God concluded that he "was sorry that he had made Saul king over Israel."[12] Again, Boyd helps us to see the quandary over such regret:

> We must wonder how the Lord could truly experience regret for making Saul king if he was absolutely certain that Saul would act the way he did. Could God genuinely confess, "I regret that I made Saul king" if he could in the same breath proclaim, "I was certain of what Saul would do when I made him king"? I do not see how. Could I genuinely regret, say, purchasing a car because it turned out to run poorly if in fact the car was running exactly as I knew it would when I purchased it? Common sense tells us that we can only regret a decision we made if the decision resulted in an outcome other than what we expected or hoped for when the decision was made.[13]

Scripture also records times when God asks questions about the future (Numbers 14:11), confronts the unexpected (Isaiah 5:2–5), gets frustrated (Exodus 4:10–15) and tests people (Genesis 22:12, 2 Chronicles 32:31). None of these make sense, so argues Boyd, if God knew beforehand what would happen. It would seem, therefore, that there are some open spaces out there and what might happen in them even perplexes God.[14] What then does this have to do with praying in the war zone?

Boyd helps us to see that an uncertain future is full of possibilities. It is a future to be embraced and filled with prayer. The future, he urges, is contestable ground and must be fought over on our knees. This future can be shaped by us. Moses is a classic example. As leader of the Israelites he was charged with bringing the people of God into the Promised Land. On the way, they proved very human indeed, scorning God and turned to idols which aroused their Creator to such anger that he wanted nothing more to do with them. This it would appear was God's plan A. Moses, however, suggested to God plan B and after a free flowing rigorous dialogue God relented.[15] In this instance it would appear Moses had genuine 'say so' in the contestable arena of what would happen to the Israelites. Moses shaped the future through prayer. It has often been said that prayer is a means by which God can influence us, but in the Moses moment we see a pray-er influencing God. Possibly this is what John Wesley had in mind when he said: "God will do nothing but in answer to prayer." Without wanting to suggest that everything hinges upon our prayer life, Walter Wink is right to suggest that "God's hands are effectively tied when we fail to pray."[16] So, in a very real sense the future is ours to create. We do have what Boyd refers to as 'say-so' in this world. God will not always unilaterally determine all things and waits for us to influence him through our prayers.

Prior to publication, some friends and colleagues of mine read this chapter and it was their view that I have come across as endorsing open theism. Frankly, I find this puzzling considering the first half of this chapter where I categorically state that at the center of the universe there seems to be a God who knows the future we will have. I have to admit though, that the open theists do raise important questions even if I do have some problems with their view on God's foreknowledge (see footnote 14). For this reason I put the brief summary of open theism alongside classical theism. I would love to find a way of reconciling these two views as I think both are healthy attempts at trying to resolve awkward questions about suffering. For the Christ soldier who believes God knows all things; past, present and future, it makes sense to spend quality time so he can whisper to our spirits, and prepare us for what lies ahead. If, that spiritual soldier is an 'open theist'; then the call to prayer is no less urgent as they are granted the privilege of influencing God as he moves to reshape the world. Either way prayer is a critical weapon of warfare not be discarded on the battlefield.

1 Ezekiel 24:15–18.
2 Isaiah 6:8–13.
3 Genesis 37:1–8.
4 Acts 27:23–26.
5 Genesis 12:2.
6 Brother Yun with Paul Hattaway, *The Heavenly Man* (London: Monarch Books; 2002), p.327.
7 Howard Bloom, *The Lucifer Principle: A Scientific Expedition into the Forces of History* (New York: Atlantic Monthly, 1995), pp.2–3.
8 A. Dillard, *Pilgrim at Tinker Creek* (New York: Harper Collins, 1974), p. 179.
9 Ron Sider is right to remind us that for many people tsunamis strike every week. He writes, "every day 30,000 children die of starvation and diseases we know how to prevent – 210,000 dead (counting only the children) every week. That means more than 52 times as many children die unnecessarily from poverty every year as those who perished in the year-end tsunami." (Prism, 2005). Sider goes on to inform us that according to the World Bank, 1.2 billion people struggle to survive on just one dollar a day. Another 1.6 billion live on less that two dollars a day.
10 Genesis 6:6.
11 Gregory A. Boyd, *God of the Possible* (Baker Books, 2000), p.55.
12 1 Samuel 15:35.

13 *God of the Possible*, p.56.
14 For all that I like Gregory Boyd's material I have to be honest that some of his arguments at this point are less than convincing. What I really appreciate about Boyd is that he strives for biblical accuracy and scriptural support. But like all of us, he sometimes attempts to squeeze too much out of certain passages. Millard Erickson cautions Boyd in questioning "whether the feeling of such pain, occasioned by God's having brought these persons into these positions implies a surprise or something that he did not know would occur. Is it the case that if I knew that something unpleasant will occur, I do not feel pain when it occurs? If we are to appeal to common sense, as Boyd does, it seems that this is not necessarily the case. For example, one may know that one's parents will someday die and that in all likelihood their deaths will precede one's own, yet grieve and feel deep pain when they actually occur. Millard Erickson, *What Does God Know?* (Zondervan, 2003) p. 21–2).
15 Exodus 32:10–14.
16 Walter Wink, *Engaging the Powers: Discernment and Resistance in a World of Domination* (Minneapolis: Fortress, 1992), p.238.

1 Richard Lovelace, *Dynamics of Spiritual Life* (Paternoster, 1981), p.392.
2 Gregory A. Boyd, *Is God to Blame?* (Downers Grove, IL: IVP, 2003), p.136.
3 *Is God to Blame?*, p.138.
4 John Ortberg, *Get Out of the Boat* (Zondervan, 2001), p.92–3.
5 *Is God to Blame?*, p.139.
6 *Is God to Blame?*, p.141.
7 Philip Yancey, *The Jesus I Never Knew* (Marshall Pickering, 1995), p.74–5.
8 Walter Wink, *Engaging the Powers: Discernment and Resistance in a World of Domination* (Minneapolis: Fortress, 1992), p.310–311.
9 Firstly, there is good debate as to whether this book is to be taken as literal historical fact or as an epic poem. Those that debate this are not liberals but those from within evangelicalism. David Atkinson, for example, a scholar whom I had the privilege of sitting under while at the evangelical Oxford college of Wycliffe Hall concludes "that an ancient folk tale was picked up and woven into this masterly *epic poem* [italics: mine]." (*The Bible Speaks Today* (IVP, 1991, p.16). Robert L. Alden, in his book *Job* (Broadman & Holman Publishers, 1993) can see arguments on both sides. He alludes to those parts of the text that speak quite specifically of Job as a historical person, for example, as 'a man from the East' (1:1–3). But Alden also notes the seeming artificiality about the numbers of cattle (1:3; 42:12) and the almost standardization in the way the tragedies were reported (1:13–19).

Given the debate as to what kind of literature this is we must be careful as to how many points we take from this complex book. To try and establish a major point about Satan or God from a book that could be a poem gives cause for pause. However, that a story may not be true is not to say that truth cannot be found in it. We just need to be careful on how much truth we try and take out of it. As a rule of thumb, if a piece of literature has a hint of poetry or parable about it, then look for the one and only main point in the poem or parable.

John Stackhouse in his book Can God Be Trusted: Faith and the Challenge of Evil (Oxford: Oxford University Press, 1998) suggests that even though Job never really got an interpretation on his sufferings he did receive the following. First, he actually does hear from God. Second, God does address Job's questions, confusions, and fears. Third, God vindicates Job in the eyes of his companions, and goes on to tell the first three that they have slandered not Job, ultimately, but God. Fourth, God restores Job's material fortunes twofold and grants him another ten children. (pages 96–7). Stackhouse concludes that Job and others in Scripture who suffered teach us that it is alright to call out to God in anger and that God is rarely offended by this action. God will respond even though he may never fully explain the rationale for what God is doing. Nonetheless, God does respond in a way that confirms and strengthens the faith of the desperate inquirer. (p.98).

10
11 Robert Clinton, *The Making of a Leader* (Navpress, 1988), p.63–6.
12 Joshua 6:17–19.
13 Gregory A. Boyd, *Satan and the Problem of Evil: Constructing a Trinitarian Warfare Theodicy* (Downers Grove, IL: IVP, 2001), p.213.

CHAPTER SIX

DEALING TO DUALISM

A PHILOSOPHER'S DREAM

Soon after becoming a God believer and follower of Jesus I began attending a local church that gave a lot to world mission and each year asked the congregation to seek God on how much we were to trust him for in our giving. In other words, this involved faith but for me the only job I could get was making glue in a paper bag factory. I had few responsibilities, no house and few expenses so in my youthful enthusiasm contributed up to half my hard earned wages to support the church missionaries. It was great being a giver for the Jesus revolution. One week I found myself in desperate need of a new pair of socks. Instead of going out to buy them I decided to apply a faith principle and ask God. I reminded him of all the promises about asking and getting and then waited for the socks to appear. Two weeks after praying I was rummaging through a second hand clothes store when the lady behind the counter took pity and gave me a second hand suit. I accepted it but muttered under my breath that God had got the orders mixed up. I didn't ask for a suit. Anyway, I searched the pockets of the suit looking for money (as you do!), and without a word of a lie, tucked away in one of the pockets was a brand new pair of socks! How they got there I have no idea. Now I'm not setting this up as a pattern for future financial management, rather, this naïve venture into faith taught me God cares about even the little items in our lives. Understandably, that episode nurtured within me a belief that God can do anything.

At the time of the sock story, I was an extremely shy and insecure person. A troubled home life, drugs, expulsion from university and a number of other factors, had reduced me to a nervous mess. I was emotionally distant and conversationally incoherent. When people approached me in church I froze, and then a nervous twitch would start up on my upper lip. I couldn't wait to get out of the place. Since then I have been a pastor, a missionary and a public speaker, forever meeting new people and speaking in front of different groups. I am staggered at what has happened in my life. I've gone from a being withered up to being a worker for God. How does that happen? It is my sure conviction that at the centre of the universe there are 'divine' helping hands, not folded or in pockets, but stretched toward us. When we say "yes, Lord" those hands go to work on us and make something beautiful out of our lives. Those hands of Jesus can take the very worst and turn it into the very best. That is what is happening in my life. And again, when I think of where I am now compared to all those years ago, I am compelled to say, "My God can do anything!" Or can he?

Some Christians get nervous when you start asking whether in fact God can do anything or if he might have chosen to limit himself as I suggested earlier. They fear we are in danger of trying to mould or shape God as if he were made of plasticine. Australian writer, Michael Frost, uses the example of Spanish artist Bartholomew Murillo to illustrate: 'In his home where he grew up, there was a picture of Jesus hanging in the living area. It was Jesus the shepherd boy and it portrayed him, in the style of the time, standing straight and tall, his shepherd's crook like a sentinel's bayonet. About his head hung the obligatory halo. Murillo detested the picture. So, one day when his family was out of the house, impetuously he took the framed painting down from the wall and went to work on it. His youthful brilliance already evident, he was able to recreate it into a new picture of Christ. Upon their return home, the Murrillos were aghast to see their Lord had been transformed. The stern unflinching face now had a lively grin. His eyes were alive with mischief. The halo had become a battered straw hat and the plastered down hair had become tousled and unruly. His crook had been transformed into a gnarled walking-stick and the limp and sad-looking lamb at Jesus' feet was now a troublesome puppy. The shepherd boy had become a lively and excited hiker in search of adventure.'[1]

In a sense, both the original artist and Bartholomew made the same mistake. They painted Jesus in line with their own personal preferences. I don't want to make the same mistake. My hope is to uncover the God of the Hebrews and of Jesus, not a God who is too small or who can turn circles into triangles and do the fantastical. I want to step away from the extremes and let God be God by defining himself. Fortunately for us, we do have a self-defining, self-revealing and self-communicating God. He has revealed himself to us in Christ and in scripture.

We have already established God is all powerful at the centre of the cosmos and without equal. Satan is not on the same footing. There is no dualism of equal forces in the universe. Satan has already been defeated through Christ's work on the cross which culminated in the resurrection. Despite knowing he is defeated, Satan is a genuine foe and remains a present power actively working against God's plans and purposes for humanity until God closes this chapter in history. Within this framework free-will agents, be they demonic or human, have 'say-so' These forces can influence and cause events and outcomes that are outside of the will of God. In this sense we are engaged in a real cosmic war with real opponents, real weapons and real casualties.

Many Christians have no difficulty with the notion of warfare or Satan, but have a problem with the idea that God may be somehow limited. Understandably, Christians want to defend the perfection and excellence of God. They rightly oppose any attempt to belittle or demean him.

We need to establish that there is no force that can exercise rule over God. God, as revealed to us, is the Lord of the Universe – supremely supreme, the Lord of Lords.[2] However this King who sits on the throne of Heaven is no typical monarch. He is also an artist and an ethicist. He designs a world of wonders and then for his 'piece de resistance' he creates human beings in his own image. As an ethicist he endows these humans with genuine free will, thereby accepting that he has limited himself. Therefore the freedom he has given his created beings can have an influence on God and on the ideal outcomes and desires he might have for them. Oxford University theologian Paul Fiddes, writes, "thus we arrive at the notion of God who freely accepts self-limitation for the sake of the freedom of his creation."[3]

God's plan to self-limit does not represent weakness. In his wisdom he chose to be limited. It is therefore true that while God can do anything, he has chosen to honour freewill which in turn has its own consequences and outcomes. In effect God can no longer do everything. He cannot decree free will for a person and at the same time dominate that person. It is therefore not helpful to think of God as one who can do anything, anywhere at anytime. God has chosen not to be this kind of God in our world. In a sense, God can no longer move "events and people around like pieces on a chess board."[4] Rather than weakness, all this says is that God has chosen to work within what he has created rather than despite what he has created. But is this God still perfect?

Our problem is that we have come to equate perfection with power, the power to do anything, anywhere at all times. But is this perfection? Is perfection getting your own way? In Jesus, we see the God of the universe taking on human form. At a certain point in his life Jesus realized that all power had been given to him.[5] So what did he do with this insight and with this power? In the very next verse, John tells us that Jesus took a towel and began to do one of the most menial and lowest jobs of the day – washing the feet of his disciples. His was a 'sandal' culture and the streets were dusty and dirty. Cleaning feet was the job of a slave, the house servant. A modern day equivalent would be that of doing the dishes or cleaning the toilets. These are the jobs no one wants to do. So Jesus realizing that all power has been given to him disrobes and dons the form of a slave. Is this not the picture of perfection? A God whose preferred way is that of weakness, suffering, and servanthood. If you want to know what perfection looks like, look at Jesus. Jesus could not control his disciples, could not control the crowds, and could not control the Jewish or Roman authorities. "The Master of the Universe," writes Philip Yancey, "would become its victim, powerless before a squad of soldiers in a garden."[6] For sure, there was much that Jesus did do, but as God, there were things he could not do. Jesus came to influence people, not coerce them. Jesus came with a light touch not a heavy hand. Jesus had a divine shyness about him, not a forceful manner. Perfection it would seem has very little to do with pyrotechnic displays of power. Jesus was no *Bruce Almighty*. Where then, did this distorted picture of perfection as control and power come from?

INTELLECTUAL INTERRUPTIONS

This 2004 Greek culture invaded New Zealand in the form of a movie and in sport. First off, we had Brad Pitt playing Achilles in the movie *Troy*. Second, during the month of August the Olympic Games in Athens filled our television screens day and night. In both of these very little mention was made of arguably one of their greatest, Plato.

Plato, the Greek philosopher, was so incensed by the shoddy treatment his teacher Socrates received at the hands of the rulers of the day he decided that nothing on this earth could be really trusted. Socrates was asked to drink a cup of poison because it was felt by the rulers of the day that he was leading the youth of Athens astray. Plato was so disgusted by the fickle nature of justice handed out to his beloved teacher that he left Athens. More than that, he left behind any notion that certain knowledge could be found in people, traditions and earthly authorities. For Plato, the things of this world were like shadows and sand – always shifting and changing and not to be trusted. He urged people to look to the heavens to see perfection. There, he declared, were ideal forms that were certain and unchangeable.

"On 13 November 354," writes Alistair McGrath, "our second intellectual was born to North African parents. It soon became clear that this child was clever, very clever. His mother was an enthusiastic Christian and dearly wanted her son to come to faith but she could not handle his difficult questions. Eventually, her son became alienated from the Christian faith charging that it lacked intellectual respectability. The young man went to Carthage to further his studies, more specifically to learn law. At that time, to progress in law you had to have a grasp of rhetoric and the Latin language, and this young man did. But while at university his interests went further than studies. He wanted to explore, to test his limits, to be free and to fall in love. So he indulged himself sensually and within a year of being at university was living with his girlfriend whom he got pregnant. He ended up being a father at the age of eighteen.

Shortly after the birth of his son he got involved in a religious sect that taught Jesus Christ was a good teacher, worth listening to but warned its followers to have nothing to do with the Old Testament. He remained in this sect for nine years, eventually accepting a teaching post at Carthage. His hope was to climb the ladder to important imperial administrative jobs in the big cities.

At this point he began to have doubts about the sect and a spiritual restlessness took root deep in his heart. As providence would have it, he was offered a good job in the city of Milan and there heard some insightful preaching at the local church which bought him to a spiritual crisis. He broke off his relationship with his partner and the sect. Then a visitor came to his house advising him that a friend had recently converted to Christianity through studying the scriptures. Soon afterward, while sitting under a tree in the garden of his house, he began to pray to God, saying he couldn't go on and needed something more in his life. As soon as these words left his lips he heard children next door playing and singing, "Take up and read! Take up and read!" He rushed indoors, opened a Bible at random, and read the verses before him: "Clothe yourselves with the Lord Jesus Christ, and do not think to gratify the desires of your lower nature" (Romans 13:14). He closed the book, and told his friends he had become a Christian.[7]

This wonderfully converted scholar became a leading thinker and writer determined to make God clear to his church and world. To assist him in this endeavour, Augustine 'Christianized' Plato:

> If those, however, who are called philosophers, happen to have said anything that is true, and agreeable to our faith, the Platonists above all, not only should we not be afraid of them, but we should even claim back for our own use what they have said, as from its unjust possessors. It is like the Egyptians, who not only had idols and heavy burdens, which the people of Israel abominated and fled from, but also vessels and ornaments of gold and silver, and fine raiment, which the people secretly appropriated for their own, and indeed better, use as they went from Egypt; and this not on their own initiative, but on God's instructions, with the Egyptians unwittingly lending them things they were not themselves making good use of.[8]

Augustine took from Plato his concept of ideal forms in the heavens and used these to describe and define God. Greek philosophy therefore became a grid to understand God,[9] who became an ideal perfect form. In the Greek mind, for something to be perfect it had to be unmoving and unchanging, a sort of static perfection. There could be no sense of change or of one thing becoming something else, as this would imply imperfection. Therefore God became the God of perfect power (omnipotence), and perfect knowledge (omniscience), all powerful and all knowing.

So what have we ended up with here? Is the God we choose to believe in the God of the philosophers, or the Hebrews and Jesus? We have already established that God chose a certain kind of world to bring into existence and in actualizing human and angelic freedom, rejected the option to coerce. As evangelical theologian Alister McGrath writes, "There are certain things which God could do *once* which can *no longer* be done."[10] God has committed himself to limitations. This picture of God has very little to do with the picture of perfection painted by the philosophers. If the God of the philosophers can fit into neat and tidy boxes, the God of the Jews and Jesus is by comparison untidy and unpredictable. If the God of the philosophers is all powerful then the God of Jesus chooses powerlessness.

Soren Kierkegaard gives us a glimpse of the self-chosen powerlessness of Jesus:

> Imagine there was a King that loved a humble maiden. She had no royal pedigree, no education, no standing in the court. She dressed in rags. She lived in a hovel. She led the ragged life of a peasant. But for reasons no one could ever quite figure out, the King fell in love with this girl, in the way Kings sometimes do. Why he should love her is beyond explaining, but love her he did. And he could not stop loving her.
>
> Then there awoke in the heart of the King an anxious thought. How was he to reveal his love to the girl? How could he bridge the chasm of station and position that separated them? His advisers, of course, would tell him to simply command her to be his queen. But power – even unlimited power – cannot command love. His advisers might suggest that the King give up this love, give his heart to a more worthy woman. But this the King will not do, cannot do.
>
> The King could try to bridge the chasm between them by elevating her to his position. He could shower her with gifts, dress her in purple and silk, have her crowned queen. But if he brought her to his palace, if he radiated the sun of his magnificence over her, if she saw all the wealth and power and pomp of his greatness, she would be overwhelmed.
>
> Every other alternative came to nothing. There was only one way. So one day the King rose, left his throne, removed his crown, relinquished his sceptre, and laid aside his royal robes. He took upon himself the life of a peasant. He dressed in rags, scratched out a living in the dirt, grovelled for food, dwelt in a hovel. He did not just take on the outward appearance of a servant, it became his actual life, his nature, his burden.[11]

The monarch refuses to command and coerce love. Instead, the King chooses the path of powerlessness as the way to woo the beloved. This is the way of God. Again Yancey assists, "I believe God insists on such restraint because no pyrotechnic displays of omnipotence will achieve the response he desires. Although power can force obedience, only love can summon a response of love, which is the one thing God wants from us and the reason he created us."[12] In my post-graduate research into the life and theology of Dietrich Bonhoeffer, the German pastor who courageously lost his life for his stand against Hitler, I came across his thoughts on the God who chooses weakness over domination:

> God lets himself be pushed out of the world on to the cross. He is weak and powerless in the world, and that is precisely the only way, in which he is with us and helps us...The Bible directs us to God's powerlessness and suffering; only the suffering God can help us.[13]

In the incarnation of Jesus, God reveals himself as powerless and dies a hideous death. In other words, God in Christ did not fit the "all powerful" formula. Unlike the God of the philosophers, the God of the Jews and of Jesus breaks the rules, acts out of character and takes us by surprise. The mere fact that God comes to a teenage girl and asks to use her womb to make his way into the world is evidence enough that he is somewhat 'left field'. This is the kind of God we need to expect in the war zone; a God who is there but at times seemingly absent, powerfully expresses himself as powerless; a God in control but whose hands are tied by other forces.

STRENGTH IN WEAKNESS

It might be argued that it is better to have an omnipotent God in the war zone to get on top of the enemy? This however, depends on whose interests you have at heart. If you are thinking about yourself and your side, then arguably it may be better that he is all powerful so you get what you want. What if we try and see things from the perspective of free will human agents who are causing mayhem and madness in the war zone? At the end of the day, what kind of God is going to win them over? And before we get to that question let us never forget that we are to be against the principalities and the powers, not people. Marva Dawn in her superb book *Powers, Weakness, and the Tabernacling of God* quotes Yoder Neufeld where the latter writes, "the critical and essential task is to maintain the irony in such warfare, and to remain deeply conscious that is always a battle for flesh and blood and never against it."[14] Back to the question: do 'flesh and blood' people prefer a God who overwhelms or woos them?

In the movie *Keeping the Faith* Ed Norton plays Brian, a Catholic Priest whose best friend Jake (Ben Stiller) is a Jewish rabbi who both have 'a thing' for the zany and charged Anna (Jenna Elfman). This tryst makes for much sexual tension which culminates in Norton declaring his love to Anna and Anna having to confess she is involved with Jake the rabbi. Brian is so devastated by this news that he seeks out the one person who can assist him in his misery, his local bartender. Here is my point. At street level those in pain would rather seek out a beaten and battered bartender than a 'polished priest or pastor'. Why? When we came back from Manila with all our hurts, deep disappointments and doubts the last thing we needed was a rescuer, a fix-it type. Rather, we searched for someone who had been there and done it, who could just sit with us in our 'seething' silence. We experienced this in Manila when we lost our little boy, Joseph. As he lay in hospital dying Ruby and I would visit our mission retreat centre and crumble into their armchairs. Colin and Janet had been through years of hardship in their previous twenty-plus years of missionary endeavour in Indonesia. They were perfect for us at this time. When we cried, they cried. When we were lost for words, they offered none. When we sat in silence, they remained still.

Jesus didn't want to suffer. He recoiled from it, and in the midst of his suffering felt absolutely forsaken. Here we see God himself as a casualty in the war zone. It was this beaten up and broken Jesus that I found so compelling in my dark forest moments. I experienced Jesus as one who had also felt the depth of the human condition. He and I connected at a profound level and this connection, this solidarity in suffering, strengthened me to transcend my circumstances and keep moving on.

It is this God that people need to hear about in the war zone. Sadly, what they often get told about is the God of the philosophers, the one who sits on his throne above and beyond, forever perfect, powerful and unchanging (immutable) despite the pain on the planet. Quite understandably, that kind of God has given rise to protest atheism.[15] The God of the philosophers does not make sense to people in pain.

This is not to suggest though that the God manifest in Jesus is simply an armchair empathizer. If we have someone who can sit with us, in time we can also look for ways to overcome and eventually oppose suffering. Just as Christ overcame all that was done to him so we too can transcend our brokenness and losses. Overcoming has nothing to do with trying to forget, nor is it about positive thinking to convince ourselves what was bad is in fact good. Rather, overcoming is inviting another life to take up residence inside us. God doesn't bring the worst into our lives in order to bring about the best, but the presence of the Holy Spirit gives us the power to squeeze something good from even the worst circumstances. God does not will evil into existence but there is a sense in which he can take all our hurts, mistakes and misery and transform this into a new beginning. The empathizer is at one and the same time an overcomer and a re-creator.

THE GOD OF THE CHRIST-SOLDIER

Is it better to have a 'commander' who can stamp authority all over the place, or a God who has a divine shyness? Which kind of God will create the best soldier or bring out the best in a soldier?

Excessively strong fathers run the risk of reducing their children to those who stay hidden in the shadows – out of sight. These children may continue to cower in the corner believing they have nothing to offer compared to their parent. If these children do emerge, they invariably end up being overly dependant on the strong parent to get things done in their lives. Either way, immaturity is the result. Likewise, believing in a God of omnipotence and dominance, can give rise to immature believers. Far from embracing life and soaring like an eagle we get passive believers, cowering in cathedrals and waiting for almighty God to do everything for them. From this arises an unhealthy dependency in and on the church. Far from a God of omnipotence strengthening the believer, the Christian is disempowered.

When, however, I think of a God who self-limits himself and chooses to invite us to participate in the fight against evil, I am empowered to be all I need to be. I come out of the dark corner empowered and eager to fight. I want to be apprenticed to this God, so I can be the best fighter possible. This I think is how Jesus saw his partnership with the Father. When he said that he only does what the Father is doing, this doesn't imply an overly dependant Jesus fearful of stepping out of line. Rather, as the New Testament scholar Tom Wright suggests, Jesus saw himself in an apprenticeship relationship with his father. Wright comments that in (John 5) "Jesus is watching [the Father] to see how it is being done, so as to do it alongside the father."[16] Like an apprentice carpenter, Jesus was co-creating with the Father. Both were about the business of building and they did it in unison, depending upon each other, opposing evil wherever it was found. There was something about the Father that had Jesus coming alongside rather than cowering, and wanting to work for good against evil. Maybe there is something about this God that also inspires and encourages us to stand up, become equipped and stride forward into the war zone to fight the 'good fight'.

1. Michael Frost, *Jesus the Fool* (Albatross, 1994), p.19.
2. Dueteronomy 10:17, 1 Timothy 6:15; Revelation 17:14, 19:16.
3. Paul S. Fiddes, *The Creative Suffering of God* Oxford, Clarendon Paperbacks, 1988), p. 33.
4. *The Creative Suffering of God*, p. 32.
5. John 13:3–4
6. Philip Yancey, *The Jesus I Never Knew* (Marshall Pickering, 1995), p.74.
7. Alistair McGrath, *A Cloud of Witnesses* (IVP, 1990), pp.23ff.
8. Augustine, *Teaching Christianity – Da Doctrina Christiana*, introduction, translation, and notes by Edmund Hill, O.P., in *The Works of St. Augustine for the Twenty-First Century*, vol.11 (Hyde Park, N.Y.: New City Press, 1996), pp.159–60.
9. In reference to the connection between Greek Philosophy and Christian Theology, Fiddes affirms "that the early Fathers of the Church recast the God of the scripture in the mould of Greek philosophy" (p.38) and further Wolfhart Pannenburg notes that it "was from Platonism, above all, that early Christian theology borrowed the conceptual tools for its reflections upon the nature of God" (Pannenburg, *Basic Questions in Theology*, Vol.1., London: SCM, 1971:122).
10. Alister McGrath, *Christian Theology: An Introduction* (Oxford, Blackwells; 1994), p.225.
11. I think I gleaned this story from Tony Campolo's *Let Me Tell You A Story* (Nashville, Word Publishing, 2000).
12. *The Jesus I Never Knew*, p.76.
13. Dietrich Bonhoeffer, *Letters & Papers from Prison* (SCM Press, 1971), p360–1.
14. Marva J. Dawn, Powers, *Weakness, and the Tabernacling of God* (Grand Rapids, MI: Eerdmans, 2001), p.130.
15. For an excellent chronicle of the rise and fall of atheism, see Alister McGrath's *The Twilight of Atheism* (NY: Doubleday, 2004).
16. Tom Wright, *John for Everyone: Part 1* (London: SPCK, 2002), p.62.

CHAPTER SEVEN

THE COURAGE TO STAND

A WOMAN'S WEAPONS

My favourite book in the Bible is Judges. I love it because the characters that fill the pages are wild people whom I believe make God's heart sing. God doesn't only choose the nice people to be his divine warriors but has an eye for those with sharp edges who can come across as loose cannons. One such character is Jael, who finding herself in a tough situation emerges as one tough lady. Jael[1] is unexpectedly and suddenly thrust into a messy war situation when Sisera arrives. Sisera, fresh from the battlefield where the war was going against him, had escaped and walked about 50 miles to Jael's place. Significantly, he is the commander of the army that has just been defeated by the Israelites. Jael is caught in a complex war zone situation. What is she to do? She knows the victorious Israelites will be on his tail trying to track him down, and anyone caught aiding and abetting him would have a lot of explaining to do. Jael brings out a woman's weapons – a big-hearted welcome (she gives him her own bed), generous hospitality (he asks for water but she gives him milk), and courage to invite him in, in the first place. To these weapons are added two more, a tent peg and a hammer!

As he lies absolutely exhausted on the bed, she drives the tent peg into his head, through his temple. This is surely one of scripture's most disturbing stories. We are told in the New Testament that all of scripture is inspired by God and is useful[2] which of course begs the question: How on earth is this chilling story of Jael useful to us today? Often, in order to understand one story, especially a complex one like this, you have to be aware of related encounters which may provide understanding.

DANCING IN THE MINEFIELD

From the files of Amnesty International comes the story of a Chilean singer who demonstrated the deeper meaning of "dancing in the minefield" (in Annette Kolodny's famous phrase). The singer Victor Juarez, was imprisoned with thousands of others in the National Stadium in Santiago when the government of Salvador Allende was overthrown by Augusto Pinochet, a career military officer and a ruthless and brutal politician. As the singer stood among the frightened and demoralized prisoners, who had been rounded up for unknown reasons, he began a solitary freedom song. A guitar was passed to him. The spirit began to blow. Soon thousands were singing this Chilean folk song with him.

As usual, the authorities were threatened by the power of the spirit moving so freely and blatantly. They seized the young man and took him away. When they returned Juarez, he was dumped in the midst of the crowd and the guitar which had been smashed to pieces, was thrown at his feet. Not only had the guitar been destroyed, but all ten of the singer's fingers had been cut off. Horrified, his fellow prisoners drew back. But the young man walked into the moat of empty space they had created, lifted his bloody hands and began to lead in another folk hymn and freedom song. Once more the spirit began to move. The people took up his new song, another Chilean folk hymn.

Predictably, the guards moved in again. This time when they brought him back there was blood trickling from his mouth. They had cut out his tongue. Many wept. Everyone was watching. For a while, the singer lay motionless. Then he stood up and began to sway. Some thought he was fainting. But then they realized his graceful, silent swaying was a dance, a dance to the beat of the song he had led them in earlier, but a song he could no longer sing. Soon they were all swaying silently with him.

When the guards came this time, they wasted no time. They shot him dead in front of all the people. But the spirit continued to blow. The beat went on. Indeed, the beat goes on today in Chile.[3]

Admittedly, the above incidents (Jael and Victor Juarez) are extraordinary. A more ordinary but no less painful 'boundary situation' for some might be discovering you have lost your job. Jesus, for example, tells the parable of the shrewd manager,[4] who on hearing that he was to lose his job, set about striking up deals with his master's creditors, thereby gaining friends for his soon to be insecure future. Luke records the efforts of the soon to be sacked manager are affirmed by his boss. I mean the story is hardly about business ethics as the man has cheated his boss so how then is this useful? And how do these two stories shed light on Jael?

SPIKING YOUR ENEMY

It is said that in the face of any crises there are usually four types of people. The first stick their heads in the sand and pretend nothing is happening; the second scratch their heads wondering what is happening; the third ask others what is happening; and then there are those that make things happen. What Jael, Victor and the sacked manager have in common is that they made something happen. They were people of daring initiative.

Jael could not bury her head in the sand and pretend that Sisera and the whole awful mess didn't exist nor waste time scratching her head. Sisera was already at her tent door. She finds herself frozen in time with an impossible situation. Her only way forward is an act of daring initiative, which renders her guilty[5] of half a dozen of God's commandments.

Dietrich Bonhoeffer, the young German pastor who opposed Nazism, knew what Jael had faced. Stacked in his life was a Sisera who went by the name of Adolf Hitler. Bonhoeffer likened Hitler to a truck swerving out of control down a street leaving victims in its wake. In the war zone of Germany, Bonhoeffer was horrified as Christians and churches refused to believe what was happening. In the spirit of Jael he finally concluded the only way to stop a runaway truck was to ram a spike into one of its wheels. As a follower of Jesus, he reluctantly joined the resistance movement with its stated aim of last resort to assassinate Hitler. In the spirit of Ehud, another in the Book of Judges who spiked a ruler, he too would commit the act of tyrannicide, the killing of a tyrant. Bonhoeffer realized that in his war zone he had to express himself as a decision maker. He had to step out into the cold hard realities of the war zone, explore all the possibilities and then commit himself to a daring venture. It was not enough to wait for someone to tell him what to do, he must decide and act for himself.

A PEOPLE OF DARING INITIATIVE

The commentator Schneider, describes Jael as one who "acts independently"[6] and one who takes "matters into their own hands."[7] She is a person of initiative and is commended for this, even if her actual deed is morally repugnant. Likewise, the 'shrewd manager' is not commended for his dishonesty but for his audacious action in a crisis. Leon Morris, in commentary on this parable, writes "even dishonest worldly people know how and when to *take decisive action* [italics: mine], much more should those who follow him [Jesus]".[8] Another commentator on the shrewd manager writes of his *incisiveness of action*[9] and stresses the challenge is "for us to have the shrewdness to recognize and *seize the opportunity* that exists in the midst of a threat."[10]

Jael took matters into her own hands, Victor Juarez stepped forward and did what he could and the shrewd manager took decisive action. All three found themselves in the crucible of harsh circumstance and seized the opportunity.

I have lived in a number of cities around the world but in our present location I think I have come across a half-truth. This is best summarized in a puzzling little story about Melvin the monk. Melvin, an absent-minded monk, took a daily walk to read his breviary. Unfortunately, Easter Sunday had extra psalms to read and Melvin walked too far – right off a cliff. Fortunately, he felt something was amiss and grabbed a tree branch. As Melvin's feet dangled 300 feet over the canyon, he frantically shouted,

"Help! Is there anyone up there?"

Suddenly the clouds parted and a loud voice boomed,

"I will help you. Are you willing to do whatever I ask?"

"Of course. What do you want me to do?"

"Let go."

"Who are you?"

"God."

"Is there anyone else up there?" [11]

This is the picture some have of God when they find themselves in a crisis. They believe that somehow it is all up to God if we are to be rescued. They think that it is in God's job description to do everything for us.

The story of God insisting 'Melvin the monk' simply let go of everything and it would be done for him, is very popular in my city. It sounds so spiritual and scriptural, but is it?

In Genesis, we are informed men and women were created in God's image. In the New Testament, we are told to be conformed to that image – which begs the question – what is that image? In John's Gospel, are we told of a God who saw the world was going to rack and ruin, so buried his head in heavenly sand and pretended nothing was happening? No! Or, when God saw his world going to the dogs, did he scratch his head and wonder what on earth was happening? No! Did he turn to the Son and ask what was happening? Wrong again. God saw the world he loved was in a huge war-like mess so he took a daring initiative and sent his Son into a world that had a reputation for killing prophets. God took the initiative and that is the image we have been stamped with. We are to be people of mighty thoughts and spirited deeds, who seize the moment, grab the opportunity, and ride the wave of daring and bold ventures.

THE WAR ON POVERTY

In 1985 we were a young family relocated from New Zealand to the urban slums of Manila. We illegally squatted on land owned by another and in doing so joined thousands of extremely poor Filipinos who were also there illegally. Our home for the next 10 years was a shack made of plywood sheets, misery, and personal pain. Since returning in 1994 we are often asked why we undertook such a venture? This question is the stuff of ethics.

Some have suggested we did what we did because it was 'in us' to do; that somehow all the forces of our background and upbringing made us into the kind of people who do such things. "Well, given your kind of history," we could almost hear some thinking, "it is no wonder you behaved in such a radical way." These people looked at my rebellious past in the hippie drug counter culture and concluded there was obviously a wild side in me and only wild people would go to the slums. This explanation breaks down when it is explained that Ruby came from a completely different background. By comparison if I was a bit wild, she was nice. The decision to go was as much hers as mine. Those of a more evangelical bent, suggest we must have heard such a clear command to 'go to the slums'. In reality, we received little or no 'guidance'. The heavens did not part and no booming voice was heard.

To be candid, this decision to go to the slums was not God's decision for us but *our decision* for God and the poor. Put simply, we acted as free-will agents. We experienced ourselves as decision makers. *We chose* between possibilities, *we explored* the option of living in a slum, *we decided* and then finally *we stepped* out into the unknown. Admittedly, other causes like our upbringing, church, faith or personality may have influenced this act. However there was no sense of coercion and no determinism other than *self*-determination. We were not acted upon but freely acted in a daring venture of initiative. We simply put up our hands and said we'd go.

This reminds me of the true account of Father Damien. In the movie *Molekai*,[12] we see him serving as a priest in the South Pacific. Leprosy was rife in the region and everyone who had contracted the disease was shipped off to an inhospitable island to fend for themselves. This played on the conscience of the Catholic Church which decided to send one of their priests. But who would go? Such an assignment was a sure death sentence. The Bishop gathered his priests together, explained the situation and simply called for volunteers. There were no flashes of light or voices. After a few minutes of silence four priests stood up and Father Damien was asked to be the first to go. He served the people on the island in an holistic way through evangelism and social action; and then like all the other inhabitants, died a leper. What struck me in his story was that he volunteered. He made a decision and put his hand up. He took initiative!

A DISCIPLE'S FREEDOM

We felt that it was up to us whether or not we went to the slums of Manila. There was a very real sense of our enjoying a d*isciple's freedom* in the matter. For some, this may appear as a contradiction or an oxymoron. A disciple by definition is one who follows, while freedom implies the opposite. Far from being 'other-determined', freedom is the notion of self-determination. There is often a paradoxical feature to scripture where seemingly opposite things are held in critical tension. While disciples do follow they are also to venture out of their own accord and act. Disciples do obey but they are to also charge ahead, decide and do. Far from discipleship being reduced to obedience, it can be expanded to include freedom to think, choose, decide and act.

Some may question whether Jesus took such initiative? In the Gospel of John, we read of Jesus saying he will lay down his life "of his *own accord* [italics: mine]."[13] Schnackenburg suggests that this speaks of "the sovereignty of the Son" and "as something decided by himself and of his own free will."[14] On the one hand, John is careful to note that Jesus lived his life as one who depended upon the Father in all things and sought only to please the Father. But, on the other hand, the Son also acted in freedom. Beasley-Murray brings these two strands that appear as seeming opposites together in describing Jesus as "the Son [who] obeyed, in freedom."[15] We too, in conformity to that image, are to go forth and live boldly. We are to be Christ-soldiers of grit and fibre, of strong resolve, who can make difficult decisions, take risks, step forward and venture out.

A vivid example of this is the story of Jonathon, the son of King Saul:,

> 2 Saul was staying on the outskirts of Gibeah under a pomegranate tree in Migron. With him were about six hundred men,
> 3 among whom was Ahijah, who was wearing an ephod. He was a son of Ichabod's brother Ahitub son of Phinehas, the son of Eli, the LORD's priest in Shiloh. No one was aware that Jonathan had left.
> 4 On each side of the pass that Jonathan intended to cross to reach the Philistine outpost was a cliff; one was called Bozez, and the other Seneh.
> 5 One cliff stood to the north toward Micmash, the other to the south toward Geba.
> 6 Jonathan said to his young armor-bearer, "Come, let's go over to the outpost of those uncircumcised fellows. Perhaps the LORD will act in our behalf. Nothing can hinder the LORD from saving, whether by many or by few."
> 7 "Do all that you have in mind," his armor-bearer said. "Go ahead; I am with you heart and soul."
> 8 Jonathan said, "Come, then; we will cross over toward the men and let them see us.
> 9 If they say to us, 'Wait there until we come to you,' we will stay where we are and

not go up to them.
10 But if they say, 'Come up to us,' we will climb up, because that will be our sign that the LORD has given them into our hands."
11 So both of them showed themselves to the Philistine outpost. "Look!" said the Philistines. "The Hebrews are crawling out of the holes they were hiding in."
12 The men of the outpost shouted to Jonathan and his armor-bearer, "Come up to us and we'll teach you a lesson." So Jonathan said to his armor-bearer, "Climb up after me; the LORD has given them into the hand of Israel."
13 Jonathan climbed up, using his hands and feet, with his armor-bearer right behind him. The Philistines fell before Jonathan, and his armor-bearer followed and killed behind him.
14 In that first attack Jonathan and his armor-bearer killed some twenty men in an area of about half an acre.

What I like about Jonathan was his declaration of "perhaps the Lord will act on our behalf." His venture was not one of certainty. He wasn't sure that it was a done deal or God's will. It was instead, a daring venture of initiative. Jonathans are urgently needed in the war zones of today. Those who can see that a hill needs to be taken, and of their own accord , step out and take an enormous risk. This is what we believed we were doing in the slums of Manila. It was our decision for God rather than his decision for us. Having said that, our decision was not made overnight, it was carefully made based on a number of principles, careful research, consultation with God, scripture and our local church.

It seems many Christians are waiting for God to do something when in fact God may be waiting for them. We get one shot at life and in this life God will do much for us but he will not do everything. I firmly believe it is time that we recapture a daring sense of initiative, where we rediscover the act of seizing the moment. We need to re-ignite the big idea of living audaciously and recklessly, summon the courage to be all that we were created to be; people who think, choose, decide, step out and act.

Soren Kierkegaard believed that we only truly experience our own existence when we act, and make significant choices. What mattered for Kierkegaard was the subjective choice, the leap of faith, a commitment to the absurd. It was not so much what you know, but how you react. Try and capture the spirit of this man's thought in the following quotations:

> It is dangerous business to arrive in eternity with possibilities that you have prevented from becoming actualities… Trusting in God, I have ventured, but I have failed – there is peace and rest and God's confidence in that. I have not ventured – it is an utterly unhappy thought, a torment for all eternity.

A person can distress the spirit by venturing too much… But a person can also distress the spirit by venturing too little. Alas, but this comes home to him only after a long time, perhaps after many years when he is living in the security he sought by avoiding danger. Now he must experience the truth that he was untrue to himself. Perhaps it does not come until old age, perhaps not until eternity. In any case, the thing to do about venturing too little is to admit humbly before God that you are coddling yourself.

We delude ourselves into thinking that to refrain from venturing is modesty, and that it must please God as humility. No, no! Not to venture means to make a fool of God – because all he is wanting is that you go forth. [16]

Here is an amazing story about an 83 year old 'shut in' who was in failing health and couldn't leave her house. Despite her circumstances she took initiative and contacted Amnesty International asking if she could assist in some way. They informed her she now had the responsibility for obtaining the release of a political prisoner in Indonesia. With pen in hand she proceeded to write countless letters to prison officials, family and government officials. After many months she received a letter from the prisoner:

> They kept seeing and hearing my name. I was lost. I was nothing to them. They had locked me away for years with no cause. But you wouldn't let them forget. Thank God for you, my woman. You kept my name alive.
>
> When they finally released me, they said my file was two inches think with correspondence. Most of it was from you. They said the file was too much trouble for just one prisoner:
>
> I owe you my life. Words can never express my thanks. May every political prisoner's life become two inches thick.[17]

This woman seized the day, she put her hand up and stepped out into the unknown. Initiative in the war zone is no respecter of age. You can be a Jonathan or a shut in, all you have to do is make a decision. Express yourself not as a waiter but as decision maker and take initiative in the war zone as a Christ-soldier.

1. Judges 4:17–24.
2. 2 Timothy 3:16
3. Leonard Sweet, *Aquachurch* (Loveland, Colo: Group Publishing, 1999) p.121f.
4. Luke 16:1–9.
5. In this respect, Jael's action echoes Bonhoeffer, when he writes, "Civil courage, in fact, can grow only out of the free responsibility of free men. Only now are the Germans beginning to discover the meaning of free responsibility. It depends on a God who demands responsible action in a bold venture of faith, and who promises forgiveness and consolation to the man *who becomes a sinner in that venture* [italics mine]." Dietrich Bonhoeffer, *Letters and Papers from Prison* (London, SCM Press; 1953, 1967 this edition), p.6.
6. Tammi J. Schneider, *Judges* (The Liturgical Press: Collegville Minnesota, 2000), p.77.
7. *Studies in Hebrew Narrative & Poetry – Judges*, p.77.
8. Leon Morris, *Luke – Tyndale New Testament Commentaries* (IVP, 1974, 1988). In further commentary on this passage Morris writes, "...the parable presents us with a steward who, faced with the loss of his employment, protected his future by calling in the bonds and getting the debtors to rewrite them so that they no longer carried interest. He looked to their gratitude to express itself by their taking him into their homes. His action put the owner in a difficult position. He would have the greatest of difficulty in establishing his claim to the original amounts now that the first bonds were destroyed. In any case he could not repudiate the steward's action without convicting himself of taking usury. It would be extremely difficult to obtain his legal rights and in the process he would convict himself of acting impiously. So, he put the best face possible on the situation and 'commended' the steward, thus securing an undeserved reputation for piety. The steward was now seen as conforming to the law of God and the owner as applauding this. *Both were acting decisively in a difficult situation* [italics: mine]."
9. John Nolland, *Luke 9:21–18:34: Word Biblical Commentary* (Word Publishers, 1993), p.802.
10. *Luke 9:21–18:34: Word Biblical Commentary*, p.803. Nolland writes, "..the story challenges all Christians to be as successful as the worldly wise in cutting their cloth according to their situation: to act committedly in the light of what we know (in knowing God in Christ) of the larger shape of reality, its moral texture, and its orientation to the future judgement." (p.803).
11. Matthew Linn, *Healing the Eight Stages of Life* (Crossroad Publishing Company, 1965) *p.55f*
12. *Molekai* – a commercial film starring Sam Neil and available at most video/DVD outlets.
13. John 10:18.
14. Rudolf Schnackenburg, *The Gospel According to John, Vol.2* (Burns & Oates, 1980), p.301.
15. George R. Beaslet-Murray, *John* in the *Word Biblical Commentary* (Nashville: Thomas Nelson Publishers, 1999), p.171.
16. *Provocations: Spiritual Writings of Kierkegaard*, ed., Charles E. Moore (The Plough Publishing House, 2002), p. 396–400.
17. Walter Wink, *The Power of the Small* (The Other Side, July – August, 1993).

CHAPTER EIGHT

REDISCOVERING OUTRAGE

STRANGE STORIES

The Hebrew Ehud was an expert assassin. The left hander painstakingly crafted a deadly eighteeen inch long double-edged sword that could be strapped inconspicuously to his right thigh. Through stealth and deception he manoeuvred his target to an isolated location, and then...

> Ehud reached with his left hand, drew the sword from his right thigh and plunged it into the king's belly. Even the handle sank in after the blade, which came out his back. Ehud did not pull the sword out, and the fat closed in over it. Then Ehud went out to the porch; he shut the doors of the upper room behind him and locked them.[1]

All of scripture, Paul informs us, is useful.[2] What then, is the use of this macabre and detailed account? Ehud killed an oppressive tyrant – in ethical circles this is known as tryannicide.[3] The killing of a tyrant however is unlikely to be something you and I will face in our lifetime. So we must look elsewhere for the usefulness of this passage and its implications for us in the war zone?

As we discovered with Jael in the previous chapter, sometimes one story can shed light on another. Take the story of Rosa Parks, an African-American living in Montgomery, Alabama in the 1950s. Parker Palmer, a Quaker tells her story: On December 1, 1955 Rosa Parks did something she was not supposed to do. She sat down at the front of a bus in one of the seats reserved for whites. This was a dangerous, daring and provocative act in a racist society. After she had sat down at the front of the bus for awhile, the police came aboard and said, "You know, if you continue to sit there, we're going to have to throw you in jail!". Rosa Parks replied, "You may do that." Now legend has it that a student came to Rosa and asked, "Why did you sit down at the front of the bus that day?"

She said, "I sat down because I was tired." She did not mean that her feet were tired. She meant that her soul was tired. She had had enough of playing by racist rules. Enough was enough![4]

Take Dietrich Bonhoeffer, whom I have previously referred to. He came from the German aristocracy but more importantly became a follower of Jesus and eventually was a pastor and teacher. He was a twin and his sister married a Jew. As Bonhoeffer came into adulthood and Hitler rose to power, it became clear that Jews were not welcome. Bonhoeffer involved himself in an illegal operation to smuggle Jews out of Germany. This clandestine activity became known as Operation Seven. He was arrested and while in prison the authorities discovered Pastor Bonhoeffer had also joined a conspiracy movement which had as one of its aims the assassination of Hitler. He did this as a follower of Jesus![5] His view was that if Hitler could be replaced with more just rulers, they might negotiate with the allies and bring the war to an end. The plot to kill Hitler failed and the plotters were rounded up and finally executed just prior to the end of the war. On the fateful day, 20 July 1944, when the plot failed, Bonhoeffer knew his days were numbered. He sat down with pen and paper and wrote a poem about his life. He entitled it *Stations on the Road to Freedom*. His words on action and suffering could very well be a creed for Christ-soldiers:

> ACTION
> Dare to do what is just, not what fancy may call for;
> Lose no time with what may be, but boldly grasp what is real.
> The world of thought is escape; freedom comes only through action.
> Step out beyond anxious waiting and into the storm of events,
> Carried only by God's command and by your own faith;
> Then will freedom exultantly cry out to welcome your spirit.
>
> SUFFERING
> Wondrous transformation! Your strong and active hands
> are tied now. Powerless, alone, you see the end of your action.
> Still, you take a deep breath and lay your struggle for justice,
> quietly and in faith, into a mightier hand.
> Just for one blissful moment, you tasted the sweetness of freedom,
> then you handed it over to God, that he might make it whole.[6]

For Bonhoeffer, like Rosa Parks, enough was enough, something had to be done. Hitler had to go. Sensitive Christians are uncomfortable with Bonhoeffer's decision, that a follower of Jesus could align himself with such a conspiracy to kill. Before we condemn Bonhoeffer though, we would do well by first examining the Master he claimed to follow. Jesus enters into the temple courts and is aghast at what he sees. With premeditated anger, he proceeds to make a whip. Full of fury and whip in hand he turns and literally turns the tables on the profiteering sellers of animals and birds for sacrifice and made his Father's house a 'den of thieves'.[7] Admittedly, Bonhoeffer was willing to commit an act of violence against another whereas Jesus was making an aggressive albeit violent prophetic protest.

THE ANTI-SOCIAL X-FACTOR

What do the stories of Ehud, Parks, Bonhoeffer and Jesus have in common? All knew something was wrong and with strong emotional conviction acted. These famous four, were all people of deep passion who expressed outrage. Ehud had seen enough. A foreign King had oppressed him and his fellow Israelites for 18 long years. Rosa Parks was tired. No more would she live by white racist rules. Bonhoeffer could no longer witness his beloved Germany and the world being shredded by a tyrant. Jesus could not stand by and watch the poor being economically oppressed in his Father's house. Enough was enough!

If we allow these stories to press in on us, we are confronted by a new set of questions. When did we last feel so strongly about something we took a stand against the crowd? When was the last time our heart broke over the things that grieve the heart of God? When were we people of deep emotion with a deep sense of outrage welling up inside?

Some will want to dispute the place of rage in religion arguing Christianity is more about compassion, serenity and appreciation. Roger Gottlieb, a Professor of Philosophy, addresses this when he writes;

> Yet it is also the case that such virtues (compassion, joy, serenity) can be used as a kind of "spiritual bypass" (in Miriam Greenspan's apt phrase) in which pleasing emotions serve as an escape from threatening social realities. If religions can teach us a great deal about the limits of a mentality that sees the need to struggle and rage everywhere, religions also need to learn the political lesson of resistance to injustice. If peace and gratitude are important, so are anger and fighting back.[8]

Admittedly, rage can easily become an obstacle to changing the attitudes of others. Angry young prophets get in the way of the good message they are trying to communicate. In this sense, anger can take over the person and I am in no way endorsing that approach. Rather, a Christ-soldier is to "wield the fire with wisdom and turn it to creative ends."[9] This approach is summed up in one of my favourite stories in the New Testament. It concerns four friends who deeply cared for their colleague, a paralytic.[10] They hear of an itinerant rabbi doing the rounds in their neighbourhood and the word is, he can heal people. Gathering up their friend they race off to the healing meeting only to be greeted by a packed house. Such was their outrage over the plight of their sick friend they dug a hole in the roof of the house where the meeting was being held to get close to the healer. In the passage it says that Jesus looked up and saw their faith. That is all very well and good, but when the owners of the house looked up, what did they see? Four strangers destroying their roof!

It has to be said that 'de-roofing' is very anti-social behaviour. Then again, what Rosa Parks, Bonhoeffer and Jesus did was also outside of the "laws of the land". All of these folk were de-roofers. They went to incredible lengths to be there for people in need. They went out on a limb to rescue people. Rosa Parks tore the roof off for African Americans. Dietrich Bonhoeffer sought to tear the roof off for Jews. Jesus tore the roof off for the poor and oppressed. This story also raises questions for us. When was the last time we went to great lengths to assist someone else in need? When did we last go out on a limb over someone else's suffering? When did we last tear the roof off?

NO MORE NICE CHRISTIANS

I lament the death of outrage. Without a sense of outrage we run the serious risk of being ordinary when God created us to be extraordinary. Outrage makes you do things that are out of the ordinary. Without it we run the risk of becoming nice people in a nice church. To be honest, that makes me want to reach for the nearest bucket. That may seem a bit harsh but we do get an echo of this in the Book of Revelation where God vomits over lukewarm believers. God only gave us 10 Commandments; there is no 11th that says, "Thou shalt be nice." Jesus, the head of the Church, is no Mr Nice Guy. Christians seem to have bought into the sickening idea that niceness is the essence of goodness. No more of this insipid niceness. A nice soldier is an oxymoron. Nice soldiers do not win wars.

John Ortberg tells the story of a woman at her kitchen sink who spots her dog in the next door neighbour's property with their pet rabbit firmly grasped in its jaws. She races out the door, leaps over the fence, prizes open the dog's jaws, grabs the rabbit, leaps over the fence again and races up to the bathroom. She runs the hot water, shampoos the rabbit's fur, blow dries it, runs down the stairs, out the door, leaps over the fence and places the rabbit inside its cage. Some hours later there is an almighty scream from next door. So again, she sprints out the door, leaps over the fence and asks, 'What's the matter?' "You will not believe it," she is told, "but two weeks ago our pet rabbit died and we buried it. But now it has come back to life again!"

Ortberg makes the point that many of us can be like the pet rabbit – all fluffy or nice on the outside but actually dead and buried on the inside. It is possible, he argues, to be buried and dead in our hearts before we're actually dead and buried in the ground. When we no longer have that fire in our bones or belly, and the lights go out on the inside, we're dead.

FOLLOW THE FIRE

So what are you outraged about? What hill will you take? Where are the front lines for you? It is my firm belief the answers lie in our past. In our past an event happened when the Holy Spirit ignited a spark in our spirits.

Many years ago, my wife and I were pastoring a church in Dunedin, New Zealand when a young girl approached Ruby in tears. She had just had an abortion and Ruby didn't quite know what to do, so she took her to an older, wiser woman who sat down with the young girl and gently took her through the crisis. Ruby watched with absolute amazement and as the older woman went to work, through the interaction a spark was lit in her own heart. She wanted to be there for women in crisis. Today, Ruby works with some of the poorest and broken women in our nation.

Another story concerns a close friend. When he was only two years old his mother became seriously ill. She was so sick he could not get through her bedroom door to see her. At one time he tried but was denied access. Today this friend has given his life to those who struggle to get inside church doors. He is so concerned about those who are not welcome in churches, or who give up on churches and exit, that he did a PhD on the subject and has written two books on the theme. Not only has he become a pastor, he continues to find new and creative ways to help people in and out of church doors.

My final story is about someone I met in March, 2005 the week before I finished writing this book. During that week I had the privilege of lecturing American University students in New Zealand on a semester study program. One young man told me of his time at West Point, on a student army training exercise. One evening they had to run miles over a bumpy road in full uniform. As he ran he was especially mindful of the fact God was running alongside. As he gazed up at all the bobbing heads in front he wondered what on earth they were holding on to, to survive the night. At that moment a spark was lit. He wanted to become an army chaplain. He is now completing a Religious Studies Degree and his next step is to become an enlisted soldier to get to know their world. After that he hopes to become an officer and chaplain.

Ruby's front lines are the broken down, drug infested, domestic violence-filled homes of South Auckland, New Zealand. For my friend, his front lines are around the walking wounded who come under 'friendly' and some times unfriendly fire in our churches. For the American student, and chaplain-in-training, it is to be there for those American servicemen and women who serve without God and without hope. In all three cases, the spark was lit in their past and all three have since fanned it into flame. I am persuaded that the secret of life is to not only follow the raging fire inside but to give yourself to the fire.

I would like to think that in giving ourselves to the flame, when others come near they might smell the smoke. When I arrive in heaven I want to go in smoking. I want to meet my Master still inflamed over the very things that burn up the heart of God. Do you know what gets you going, what lights your fire? If you get angry over the rights or plights of others, who are they? What stirs within? What gets your blood boiling? What is there about this sick and suffering planet that keeps you up at night? When people come asking how best they can get involved in the war zone my reflex answer is: follow your fire!

---

1 Judges 3:12–30
2 2 Timothy 3:16
3 Jehu (2 Kings 9:21–37) provides another possible precedent to tryannicide. Further, the New Testament call to "obey God rather than man" (Acts 5:29) may also echo an extreme response to an unjust state. Church history informs us that Thomas Aquinas, John Calvin, John Knox, and perhaps even Martin Luther thought that private citizens could commit such a deed. John Stott writes, "we cannot interpret Jesus' command not to resist evil as an absolute prohibition of the use of force, unless we are prepared to say that the Bible contradicts itself and the apostles misunderstood Jesus...Romans 13 must not be twisted, however, to justify the institutionalized violence of an oppressive regime." John Stott, *The Incomparable Christ* (Leicester: IVP, 2001), p.139. But Stott is also clear that an

individual is prohibited from taking the law into their own hands but to see punishment as God's prerogative.
4   Parker Palmer, *Let Your Life Speak: Listening for the Voice of Vocation* (Jossy-Bass, 2000), p.30ff.
5   In a conversation with Bishop Bell, Bonhoeffer is reported as saying, "If we claim to be Christians, there is no room for expediency. Hitler is the Antichrist. Therefore we must go on with our work and eliminate him whether he be successful or not." (Bethge 1970:626--7). In his own conversation with Bonhoeffer, Bethge, hears Bonhoeffer "pleading the need to assassinate Hitler" (Bethge 1970:659)
6   Translated from Widerstand und Ergebung, pp.403–4, as cited in *A Testament To Freedom: The Essential Writings of Dietrich Bonhoeffer*, ed. Geffrey B. Kelly and F. Burton Nelson (San Fransico: HarperSanFransico, 1990), pp.542–43.
7   John 2:13–17
8   Roger S. Gottlieb, *Joining Hands: Politics and Religion Together for Social Change* (Cambridge: Westview Press, 2002), p.52.
9   This is the thesis of a recent book by Robert Thurman entitled *Anger* (NY: Oxford University Press, 2005).
10 Mark 2:1–5

www.ingramcontent.com/pod-product-compliance
Lightning Source LLC
Chambersburg PA
CBHW052028290426
44112CB00014B/2429